THE GHOSTS OF RICHMOND

...AND NEARBY ENVIRONS

by L. B. Taylor, Jr.

Fourth Printing
1995

Photographs by the Author
Illustrations by Isobel Pettengell Donovan
Design by Howell/Oller Design

Copyright © 1985 by L. B. Taylor, Jr.
Printed in the U.S.A. by Progress Printing Co., Inc.

ISBN-0-9628271-7-7

CONTENTS

ACKNOWLEDGEMENTS

The author is indebted to a number of people and organizations for their help in the preparation of this book. These include the reference folks at the Richmond Public Library, the Virginia State Library and the Valentine Museum. Of particular aid were: Joe Palka of radio station WRVA; Sergei Troubetzkoy of the Petersburg tourist office; "Susie" Peters of the Virginia Historical Landmarks Commission; and Sarah Sartain of the Virginia Historical Society. Appreciation goes, too, to Sarah Lockwood, who graciously allowed the reprinting of her fine poem, "The First Tenant." A very special thanks is extended to Ann Black, researcher extraordinaire, whose enthusiastic efforts uncovered a number of fruitful leads. Finally, the author is most appreciative of the courtesies and cooperation extended him by the many fine people interviewed for this book.

INTRODUCTION

First, a personal note to set the record straight. The purpose of this book is not to build a case for or against the existence of ghosts. Do they exist? I cannot answer that, despite the fact that this is my third book on the subject and I have done personal research on at least 75 cases of hauntings, and have read extensively of hundreds of others. I have never personally experienced an ethereal presence. I have stood in rooms where ghosts allegedly stood; I have sat in "their" chairs and lain down on their beds. I have stalked through cemetaries beneath a full moon; tramped through dark, dank and musty cellars; and become entwined in the cobwebs of secret passageways. Yet I have never heard a single mysterious footstep, or glimpsed even the hint of a wispy apparition.

The closest I came was the time when, at the generous invitation of Sue Thompson of Tuckahoe Plantation, I visited that historic plantation and was alone upstairs photographing one of the bedrooms while Sue excused herself to tend to some chores in the kitchen far below. As I stood in the bedroom I heard the soft chords of a piano being played, and I felt a chill run down the back of my neck. As it turned out, Sue had played a little trick on me. It was she at the piano, and I have to admit the mixture of the melodic strains and my imagination had me going for awhile.

All this is not to say, however, that I disbelieve in spirits. That would be rather presumptious. But I can tell you this. I do believe in the sincerity of the scores of people I have interviewed who claim *they* saw, felt or heard ghosts.

What exactly are ghosts? No one knows for sure. Hans Holzer, who has written several books on the subject, says a ghost, "appears to be a surviving emotional memory of someone who has died traumatically, and usually tragically, but is unaware of his (or her) death." Other psychic experts have defined ghosts as apparitions of dead persons. Apparitions, in turn, are visual paranormal appearances, generally spontaneous, that suggest the real presence of someone distant or dead. However, a ghost does not have to take the form of an apparition. In other words, some ghosts may be heard or felt and not seen, through such common manifestations as footsteps, bangings on walls, rocking in rocking chairs, moanings and sobbings, even voices.

Hauntings have been described as paranormal phenomena associated with a certain location, such as a house or building. Such phenomena generally are attributed to the activity of discarnate, or disembodied, spirits. And the experts say now that, based on a considerable amount of investigative evidence, ghosts represent actual physical phenomena and are not hallucinatory.

Historically, tales of ghosts, wraiths, banshees and haunted houses have been recorded for centuries. The chain-rattling fictional ghost in Charles Dickens' "A Christmas Carol," for example, reportedly was derived from an allegedly true experience recorded by the Roman scholar, Pliny the Younger.

Of course, a certain percentage of ghostly incidents can be rationally explained. Old houses are prone to make creaking noises in the dead of night that may be misinterpreted. Undoubtedly, some people, their imaginations running at high pitch, may have perceived something supernatural that actually was a patch of smoke, gas, fog or haze that had taken the rough form of a human being.

The glare of sunlight, or moonlight on a distant window at just the right angle can play tricks on the eyes at times. Books flying across a room could have been propelled by a devilish prankster. And surely, many tales, spawned centuries ago in an era more prone to superstition, probably have been considerably embellished and exaggerated in their passing through the years from one generation to another.

Such common sense answers can solve most mysteries, but not all. Some, including a number described in this volume, defy explanation. And who are we, being mere mortals, to say that there is not a great realm of the unexplored that lies just beyond the reach of most of us. Manifestations of true psychic phenomena are too frequent and too well documented scientifically in many cases to be dismissed without further examination and understanding.

In our technological age such inexplicable occurrences may be hard to accept, but even the sternest skeptic should beware that there is not some sort of shadowy perimeter, as yet unattainable, that someday may be brought into sharper focus. How can anyone say for certain it does not exist; that ghosts do not exist?

Perhaps the words of that great craftsman of the mysterious, H. P. Lovecraft, sum it up best. In his introductory paragraph to the short story, "The Tomb," he wrote: "It is an unfortunate fact that the bulk of humanity is too limited in its mental vision to weigh with patience and intelligence those isolated phenomena, seen and felt only by a psychologically sensitive few, which lie outside its common experience. Men of broader intellect know that there is no sharp distinction betwixt the real and the unreal; that all things appear as they do only by virtue of the delicate individual physical and mental media through which we are made conscious of them; but the prosaic materialism of the majority condemns as madness the flashes of supersight which penetrate the common veil of obvious empricism."

But we may be getting too serious. As I said, the purpose of this book is not to make a believer or a disbeliever out of the reader. The purpose is, simply, to entertain. Some of the stories you will find in these pages are sketchy in detail and folklorian in nature. Others are well documented and attested to. All tell of hauntings in one form or another.

In the collection and retelling of these tales, I have endeavored to add some historical flavor which, it is hoped, will prove interesting. Many of the houses herein are well known. A few of the ghosts are well known, such as those at the Governor's Mansion and the Glasgow House. But even here my research has turned up fresh anecdotes and vignettes. Many of the legends lay lost in scrapbooks and memories; some in faded newspaper clippings of 50 and even 100 or more years ago.

There are, in all, more than 30 ghost stories here, but even this is by no means an all-inclusive list. There are surely many others, for Richmond is blessed, or cursed, depending upon how you view it, with a plethora of spirits. Experts contend this is because so much history has taken place in and around the city, and there are so many old houses still standing.

Richmond also is the home, at least for much of his life, of Edgar Allan Poe, the brilliant master of the morbid and the macabre. You will find, heading each chapter, a short quote from one of his dark works. It sets the mood.

And so, read on and enjoy — if you dare!

THE FIRST TENANT

by Sarah Lockwood
Richmond, Virginia

"The state of mind of ghosts may be similar to that of someone in delirium or high fever: a disconnection of the will and inability to distinguish between reality and dream."
—*The Occult* by Colin Wilson

She does not know what sin, heavy or small,
has held her here where dust lies white and still
along the railing and the rotting sill —
white dust her fingers' touch cannot make fall.
Sometimes among the shadows in the hall,
where a will draws her which is not her will,
She meets a face that seems to wish her ill,
but whose it was, she cannot recall.
Sometimes through broken panes she feels the air
of summer and remembers, very near
the house were roses — that their scent was sweet.
Once, living people passed her on the stair.
She could not see them, but she felt their fear
and hoped they were the last that she would meet.

C H A P T E R 1

THE LOST TREASURE OF WHICHELLO

"We had passed through walls of piled bones, with casks and puncheons intermingling, into the inmost recesses of the catacombs."
— *The Cask of Amontillado*

Mr. and Mrs. J. Donald DeVilbiss, who quietly celebrated their 50th wedding anniversary in November 1984, are gracious hosts who take obvious pride in showing their historic house at 9602 River Road on the outskirts of Richmond. It is subtly furnished with period pieces harmonious with the time it was built.

In the parlor to the right as you enter the house on the main floor is a large fireplace — there is one in nearly every room, in fact. And just to the right is an area once distinguished with elaborate wainscotting no longer visible. It is in this room that the legends persist. One is that the skeletal remains of a former owner are buried seven feet beneath the fireplace. The other is that treasure is secreted either somewhere in the structure or on its grounds, hence the reason for the missing wainscotting. Fortune hunters ripped it out years ago in a desperate search for the lost loot.

For this house is the famous Whichello.

Although the DeVilbisses say no one has gone into the history of the property thoroughly, quite a bit is known about Whichello, or the "Tall House," as it also has been called. The land on which it sits is believed to have been owned by the Randolphs of Tuckahoe. One of the family members gave this tract to his French barber, a man named Druin, who in turn passed it on to his daughter, Catherine Woodward, who built the house in 1827 at a cost of $2,000.

It has a center plan frame structure with a symmetrical, five-bay facade, and exterior end chimneys of random American bond. It stands a full two stories and includes a basement and a fully finished loft. There are two rooms on each floor opening onto a center hall. Walls are nearly a foot thick, with the exterior clapboard hung on brick and plaster.

From its earliest days, apparently, Whichello was used as a tavern for those traveling between Richmond and Charlottesville or Lynchburg. Mrs. DeVilbiss believes it primarily was a rest stop for drinking and eating rather than lodging. She reasons it was too close to Richmond for anyone coming or leaving the city to spend the night. A few miles down the road is Powell's Tavern.

After a few years, Catherine Woodward's daughter, Eliza Anne Woodward Winston, sold the house. There are conflicting accounts as to when this was done. Most say it was in

1838, although there are references to its sale in 1845. In either event, the new owner was an Englishman of questionable reputation named Richard Whichello who had arrived in the area by "sailing up the James River."

As owner and operator of the tavern, Whichello is said to have accumulated wealth, according to one old report, which "was not come by in manners befitting a Christian gentleman." He was described as being miserly and cruel to his slaves. And, it was rumored, he ran games of chance, perhaps including cock fighting, that were not always honest and above board. There is one reference to him as being the type of man who had "a willingness to turn a penny by whatsoever means. . . ."

Here, the story is picked up by A. H. Moncure, who claimed he was born in the house, probably sometime during the Civil War or early post war years. Moncure was quoted in a feature article written more than half a century ago when he then was "well advanced in years." This is what he had to say:

". . . One night about dusk in the year 1850, a cattle drover from the valley region to the West arrived at the tavern with a herd which he bedded in the corrals near the inn, and there he stayed overnight. The next day he continued into the Southern capitol, and sold his cattle, returning later to again spend the night with tavern keeper Whichello.

"After dinner that night. . . Whichello invited his guest to accompany him to the 'country store' which was in reality a crossroads barroom just a few steps from the tavern. There the two men had some drinks and it was reported that Whichello and the drover became engrossed in a poker game. Anyway, the result was that Whichello went home richer by the amount Richmond dealers paid for a herd of prime cattle, and the drover from the valley went to bed 'broke.'

"In the morning attendants found the inn keeper on the floor of his bedroom, brutally murdered, with his head beaten in with an axe. The drover was gone, so was his old red and white horse and all of the money Whichello was supposed to have had with him the night before. No trace was ever found of the cattleman, and no other solution for the tavern owner's death has ever been set forth."

Other sources say that the man's sudden death caused for what few friends he had, a curious problem. Where should they bury him? They were afraid that if his body was interred in a cemetary that the slaves he had so harshly mistreated might dig up his remains and "treat it to varied indignities in retaliation."

Mr. Moncure tells what happened: ". . . That was a problem and this is the way it was solved. The friends secretly dug a hole along side the east chimney of the old tavern. Then, from this hole they tunneled to beneath the great brick chimney, and then shoved the coffin into the tunnel until it rested under the stack. That is Whichello's tomb, and from that fact, which later gained circulation, arose many of the reports of the ghost of the old owner returning to guard the treasure which his killer could not find, and which to this day is believed buried around the building."

The stories of the hidden cache of treasure have persisted, and there have been a number of fruitless searches for it through the years. At some point, the fireplace containing Whichello's remains was dug into, and the wall adjacent to it was ripped apart.

One of the most intriguing incidents was recalled by Mrs. Joseph Crenshaw, who ran a tea shop in the house in the 1930s. "Many attempts have been made to find the reputed treasure of the man," she stated, "and some tall tales are told, such as the one an old Negro told me. 'Uncle John' came to me one day and said he had a device which could locate all kinds of metal, but which wasn't any good for papers, and (he) wanted to try it out on the old Whichello hoard. He dug in what is now the kitchen. . . But alas, no riches, unless one count the richness of the yarn old 'Uncle John' spun me, a treasure.

"The old colored man assured me that no less than three times had he struck the very box which enclosed the wealth, only to have the 'spirit trove' vanish as such troves are said to do because the digger could not restrain an ejaculation or refrain from speaking at his good fortune.

" 'You really saw it, Uncle John?' I asked. 'I sure did, deed I did,' " Mrs. Crenshaw says he told her. "Each time, he said it sank down further out of sight, and the holes filled with water. This last is true enough. The holes in the old kitchen were veritable wells, and have had to be cemented over, the water flowing into them as fast as shovels made an opening."

While Mrs. Crenshaw may have had some difficulty believing Uncle John's story, even if it was told to her in dead seriousness, she nevertheless began to feel the house was haunted. For one thing, visitors to the tea room began to complain of a "feeling." It became so strong to some of them that they left their ordered refreshments before enjoying them and rushed out of the house.

Then there was the mysterious clicking noise that wouldn't go away. Mrs. Crenshaw said it sounded like an invisible telegraph key, and it seemed to follow her throughout the house from room to room. Her maid heard it, too. Says Mrs. Crenshaw: "No matter what room I went into, immediately the strange click was there, too. I told the maid it was an electric wire, but I knew that if it had been, the house would have burned up long ago.

"I became interested in the traditions and legends of the house," Mrs. Crenshaw said, "and began to wonder on my own account what did cause so many strange incidents. One day in a spirit of daring, I braved the ridicule of my husband and friends, and decided to put my problems up to Lady Wonder, that fortune telling horse on the Petersburg Pike.

"After a few trivial questions, I said: 'Lady, is there treasure in my house?' The horse answered by spelling out the affirmative. 'Where is it?' was my next query. The horse spelled out the word 'Chimney,' and then I dared to ask again (dared for these questions are only answered when properly accompanied by the nominal amount the horse's owner collects) 'Which chimney?'

"This time, without hesitancy, the animal spelled out 'East,' which is true according to all the legends. My next try was at a more definite location, and the horse's answer was to spell out 'ten feet.' Returning home, you may be sure I eyed that fireplace and chimney many times, but I never did have faith enough to go ahead and tear up the property."

Mrs. Crenshaw continued her narrative: "The news

(about the ghost) soon spread and I received several requests from Richmonders and others interested in that sort of phenomena to hold a meeting in the old house. All of these I granted, and admit that I became intensely interested myself. The first group came out and we were sitting around the table in the tea room, the lights were all on and the fire in the fireplace added to the cheeriness. One of my guests, a well known Richmond woman, began to speak of a 'little girl' visitor we had with us. She said the little girl was giving a flower to one of the other women. Then she was gone, and the woman indicated admitted the description fitted her little niece. This was all done with the lights on and not a bit of gruesomeness.

"Next, the medium, if that was what she is called, turned to me and said an old Negro mammy was beside me. She described her and told how her head kerchief was tied in a peculiar way. It was my mother's old mammy who had taken care of me as a child. The woman said how glad the spirit seemed to have me know that she was with me again. Yes, it was Sabra all right, and this only added to my puzzlement.

"At last I asked this woman if she had noticed a queer feeling upon entering my tea room, and she said: 'Why yes, as soon as I arrived. Didn't you see me stop at the door?' I replied that I had noticed her delay in entering, and then she added: 'That was because there was a man standing just behind you. He was dressed in hunting clothes and seemed to live here.' That was my first actual contact with Richard Whichello's ghost. Since then, several others have told me of seeing the apparition, and each time it has been clothed in his hunting togs."

At another seance held in the house, Mrs. Crenshaw said the following letter in spirit writing was "materialized" at the sitting: "My treasure is not in the house, but in the yard. You should look in the backyard about 100 feet away from the house and marked by a little (here the ghost grew descriptive and drew what appears to be a small board fence on the paper) and it is about five feet under the earth. You should look toward the east when leaving the back steps and count until told to stop — then go back three paces." The writing, scrawled in a wild scribble, was signed with the initials "W. R. W."

And thus is the chronicle of the ghost of Whichello. Mr. and Mrs. J. G. Holt, who owned the property in the mid-1930s, said they never saw anything out of the ordinary in the house, "That is," Mrs. Holt added, "except evidence of where others have sought for the old treasure. Our basement floor was all dug up and we had to put in a new cement one, and the old fireplaces do look as though they had been pried apart in spots and new wood inserted in places to cover up holes made by treasure hunters.

"But the nearest we've come to being visited by Whichello in the spirit is a dream a brother of mine had one night. He did dream that there was buried riches here..."

Nor have the DeVilbisses encountered any forms of psychic phenomena in their more than 30 years in the house. "I'm afraid I'm too practical for that," Mrs. DeVilbiss says. Her husband notes that they did once hear strange noises in the chimney, but took out some pieces of it to investigate and found a nest of flying squirrels.

So, one may ask today, has the ghost of Richard Whichello given up in his quest for being avenged? Or is he finally satisfied that his ill-gotten treasure is safe at last from those who so desperately sought to find it? Or will he yet be heard and seen again, should some future tenant begin the search anew?

The words of Mrs. Crenshaw, uttered more than 50 years ago, may well be the most prophetic: "There's something supernatural about that place," she said, "any many are the people who have confirmed my opinion."

C　H　A　P　T　E　R　2

THE ETHEREAL MYSTIQUE OF "MARTHA"

"And she said to me . . . tranquilly dying, that because of what I had done for the comfort of her spirit she would watch over me in that spirit when departed."

— *Eleonora*

When Ellis and Pattie Grady moved in early 1983 into the old house off Winterpock Road in Chesterfield County known as Physic Hill, they knew little about its past history and nothing of the ethereal presence which was said to haunt it. It didn't take them long to find out for themselves, however.

It began with the lights on the upper floor. "We have three floors in the house," Pattie explains. "We have an English basement which we use as a kitchen and a den. Our master bedroom and the parlor are on the first floor, and other bedrooms are upstairs. The lights upstairs would dim for no apparent reason, then they would later come back up to their full brilliance. I couldn't explain it then, and I can't today," she says. "These are tiny candle bulbs, though, and they give the appearance of a chandelier, so they are a little spooky anyway."

Next, it was the pictures upstairs. They would fall off the wall. Pattie would replace them, only to find them on the floor again the next time she went in the room. "I wasn't really scared or anything," she says, "but after awhile you begin to wonder what is happening." Later, she began hearing footsteps over the top of the master bedroom. "They were heavy, and they sounded like human footsteps," she adds, emphasizing that they were real and not imagined sounds. Yet, each time the Gradys looked for a logical source, they found nothing.

Then one day Pattie and Ellis found the bed in the upstairs guest room completely apart with the mattress on the floor. Ellis looked for a broken or loose part, but couldn't find one.

It was as if someone, something, was not satisfied with the arrangement of the bed in the room, or perhaps was unhappy with the way the Gradys had decorated Physic Hill, and was venting their irritation. Meanwhile, the distinct footsteps persisted. It sounded as if a person were walking across the upstairs bedroom over to a window.

And there have been other "incidents." On Christmas Day 1983, there was no hot water in the sink faucet in the upstairs bathroom. Ellis couldn't find the problem. Strangely, however, the same pipe which carried hot water for the sink also brought it to the shower, and the shower worked fine! On at least two occasions the Gradys have found curtains down and sitting on the floor. "Yet we never found anything loose or broken, and the storm windows would have prevented a wind from blowing them down," Pattie says.

Her interest piqued by all that was occurring, Pattie began researching the origins of the house and its earlier occupants. Physic Hill, she learned, is an historic plantation in the Winterpock area of the county. The house is a one-and-a-half-story L-plan structure, built in two stages. It is thought that Dr. John R. Walke, a physician from Amelia County, erected the first section in 1815, and that the side-passage wing was added in 1825. The house is set on a high English basement with three-course American bond. The north chimney, the mantels in the newer section, the front door and stairway, and the pine floors all are original.

The present basement area was once a brick-walled root cellar. There is a local legend that Dr. Walke used it to incarcerate and discipline unruly slaves from Walke's Quarter. It also is told that slaves were brought there to be examined by the doctor prior to their being sold at public auction at Physic Hill. The auction block said to have been used there is on exhibit on the grounds of Chesterfield Courthouse.

The house was named for a succession of physicians who lived there over the years. Digging further into county archives, Pattie learned that Dr. Walke was born about 1790 and married Martha Branch, daughter of Thomas Branch of Willow Hill. The Walke family graveyard is located southeast of the house. Within sight of the upstairs bedroom window is a grave marked with a high, weathered headstone bearing the inscription: "Sacred to the memory of Martha B. Walke, who died 19th March, 1841. Aged 52 years and 6 months. She walked with God."

"It is the only marked stone on the plantation," says Pattie, who now believes the spirit which resides in the house is Martha. "I almost feel like I know her, and I'm not afraid. She hasn't done bad things, mostly what I would call pranks. I have decided we can live in peaceful coexistence. In fact, Ellis and I have a belief that an old home is never really owned by anyone. It is loaned to those who love and care for it and it should be shared. But I can't tell you why Martha is here. I wasn't able to find out much about her death. She could have died violently, and that's why she's come back."

Or, it is possible that she was angry with her husband, who married twice after her death, each time bringing his new bride to Physic Hill. Things did quiet down for awhile after the Gradys found an original painting of John Walke owned by one of his descendants. They had it photographed and placed the picture above the fireplace in the parlor. Pattie speculated at the time that since they were "together" again, maybe Martha would stay settled.

But such was not the case. The Gradys had the house painted in September 1984. Two painters came out on the 17th to begin work, and Ellis, Pattie and their two children were all out for the day. The next day Pattie casually mentioned to one of the men that he was painting near the ghost's window, and the painter suddenly appeared visibly upset. He told Pattie that the previous day, near dusk, while working on the end of the house near "Martha's room," he saw a lady three different times standing at the window. She did not speak, but just watched him. Then, as quickly as she appeared, she vanished and was not seen again. The painter described her in detail. She had long brown hair which came down to her shoulders in ringlets. She had a large piece of jewelry "at her neck."

"At first, I thought he meant a necklace," Pattie says, "but he thought it was more like a broach. This makes more sense because women in the 19th century often wore broaches." The painter said the woman appeared to be in her late forties or early fifties. She was slender, and she was wearing a dress with puffed sleeves.

"I told him that was our ghost," Pattie says. "Actually, I was kind of put out about this, because in all the time we've lived in the house and heard all the noises and picked up after her, she had never shown her face. And here, she appears to a perfect stranger. Maybe she knew we were away and she wanted to see what was going on."

There is an intriguing footnote to this episode. In her continuing search into the history of the house and the people who lived there, Pattie learned of a Walke descendant living in New York who had a portrait of Martha's daughter. It was painted in 1838. She obtained a photograph of the painting. It was of a gaunt young woman closely fitting the description that the painter had given of the vision he had seen in the upstairs window. And, the woman in the portrait was wearing a dress — with puffed sleeves!

LOST LOVE
IN JACKSON WARD

"The greater part of the fearful night had worn away, and she who had been dead once again stirred."

— *Ligeia*

"It was past midnight and the November wind was damp and chilling to the bone. The sky was overclouded and the gloom of the night was intensified by the absence of all pedestrians except myself and the messenger who was conducting me to the bedside of some poor sufferer in the sparsely settled section of Richmond known as 'way out in Jackson Ward.' "

It was with these words that Dr. C. A. Bryce, a respected general practitioner of medicine, began the extraordinary story of his singular experience, more than seven years earlier, in an article in the Richmond *Times-Dispatch* on Sunday, January 23, 1921.

He had been called on at a late hour by a man who asked him to come to Jackson Ward to treat a patient. The two were walking to the patient's residence when something strange occurred. In Dr. Bryce's words: "I noticed that after going a few blocks he started to turn into another street leading rather away from the most direct route to the point for which we had started."

Bryce asked why they were going out of their way and the man replied that he did not like to pass by an old house in the next block late at night. "They say it's haunted," he managed to say, but then admitted that he had not personally experienced any supernatural manifestations. Bryce, curious, and also anxious to reach his patient, get on with the task at hand, and then get home to bed, persuaded the man to walk by the house.

"We came to it almost in the middle of the next block," Bryce recalled, "and a glance at the tall old wooden building with two bushy cedars in front of the porch and almost obstructing the view from the lower windows was enough to attract my attention and tell me that this was most likely the house he dreaded to pass after dark. There, deserted, stood this lonesome relic of a home. Its front door was half open and the sash gone from an upper window while the gentle slamming of an inside door on the upper floor added to the feeling of depression that seemed at the moment almost to overpower me."

Bryce went on to treat his patient, but, intrigued, stopped by the old house again on his way home, alone. He continued his narrative: "It was late at night and the town was asleep — no living soul passing, and the moonlight completely obscured by a clouded sky. I had only gazed at the open door and window for a few minutes when I began to think I actually saw a small, white object moving around the porch floor. Before I could make out what it was, it disappeared, and I concluded that possibly I had not seen anything except of my own creation."

Bryce passed by the house several times after that, always pausing, but never seeing or hearing anything out of the ordinary. Then, about two years after he had first heard of the house, he happened to be walking by sometime after one in the morning when an inexplicable incident unnerved him.

"Earlier in the night we had had a thunderstorm, but now the clouds were shifting, and every now and then the moon would shine brightly between rifts of floating cloud. By some strange coincidence I happened to be opposite the old deserted house just as a brilliant gleam of moonlight fell upon door and windows, and as I cast my eyes up toward the sashes opening in the upper story I beheld the face of a young girl. She was clad in her night clothes, and the wind was waving her hair as it blew fitfully through the open sash.

"There was no guesswork about what I saw — the features

were clear and distinct and it was a face that I would have recognized again anywhere and one that I can recall in every line to this day. Before I could utter an exclamation, the apparition was gone and I never saw it again."

The next day, "to make sure that it might not have been a material being," Bryce took a friend to explore the house. He wrote that it was evident that no human being had been in the place for a great length of time because layers of dust laid undisturbed in all the rooms. Bryce was bewildered. He could offer no rational explanation for his vision, but neither was he willing to call it a ghost. As he put it, "I felt that the face was not the work of my imagining mind, but a veritable picture thrown upon my retina at some former time and reproduced in memory, or then and there, perceived from some substance in the window."

Absorbed by the mystery, Bryce questioned neighbors and old timers about the house and its last known occupants. He found only that "three foreigners" had lived there for a short time some years ago. They had kept mostly to themselves, and had departed abruptly without saying a word to anyone.

Five years passed before he learned more. Then he was called one day to see a sick old black man who lived, hermit-like, in a little cabin in the rear of a lot adjacent to the deserted house. The man was past 70, and Bryce recognized him from having treated him once before, several years earlier. Bryce remembered because the man had paid him with a gold French coin. Highly unusual. Nor could the man satisfactorily explain how he came to have the coin in his possession.

Bryce asked him about the former occupants of the old house, and the man at first was reluctant to talk. But after some coaxing, he relented and began to fill in some pieces of the puzzle Bryce had long sought to solve.

This is what he told the doctor: "Many years ago when the cornfields were all about where these houses and streets are now, three or four big frame houses were standing out in these fields, and this (the deserted house) was one of them. I was a boy then and this house became vacant and was closed for a year or two, until one day I noticed that people were in it.

"My mother lived in this very cabin then, and in a few days after these people had moved in, a lady came down to see her and asked her to come up to the house as she wanted to see about employing her. My mother found that the family was a gentleman, his wife and daughter, and they had three women servants that they brought with them from where they came. They were rich people and hired my mother and me, besides keeping the three women they had. They were foreigners, for when they talked to each other, we could not understand them, but their servants could."

The old man continued his tale: "They didn't go out on the streets much, but sometimes would send for a carriage and be driven out, mostly at night. Their rooms were beautifully furnished and they wore very fine clothing and had plenty of jewelry and everything else which they wanted.

"The young lady was very pretty and she was the only one that ever went out on the streets much. She would take long walks every day or two by herself. One day her father called me in his room and asked me: 'Petaire (my name is Peter but he always called me Petaire), have you seen any man walking with my daughter any time?'

"I said, 'no, sir,' and I hadn't. But I knew trouble was coming if he was that suspicious, and sure enough, one day I saw a finely dressed, handsome man meet her in the Capitol Square, and they walked along together slowly talking in their language I couldn't understand, but anybody could see they were lovers.

"Twant long after that before I saw this same man come up to the house and knock at the door. I said to myself he ain't going to get a welcome from the boss, but Miss Josephine met him herself and begged him to go back before anyone saw him. I never did know how it all happened, but her father came to the door and invited him in, and then there were fierce words, and he took his leave. The servants told my mother that the young man asked for satisfaction as he was leaving, and her father told him he would meet him in New Orleans. They said that meant a duel.

Bryce, fascinated, urged the old hermit to go on. "In a few days her father left to be gone a week or two," he said, "and when he left, Miss Josephine took to her bed. Her father did not come back, but one day when she was reading the paper she turned mighty pale and just fell over in a dead faint. Her mother grabbed up the paper and screamed like somebody wild.

"I suppose the young man was killed, maybe both of them, but that was all I ever heard of either of the men. One morning the mother called us all into Miss Josephine's room, and she was lying in bed and smiling and talking out of her head. We could see that she was dying and just before she went she said, 'tell Henri I'll always be waiting for him at the window.' She took one long breath and was gone."

Bryce said that the old man told him they shipped Miss Josephine's body away for burial, and that her mother and the servants packed up and left within a few days. He added that for a long time the old house stood deserted, the only sounds ever heard from it being the creaking of shutters or slamming of doors as the wind swept through its empty halls.

As the years passed, the house became known as haunted for, as Dr. Bryce experienced, others, too, reported seeing the wraith-like face of a beautiful young woman peering out of an upstairs window as if she were expecting the arrival of a long-lost suitor.

Who were the mysterious foreigners and what really happened to them? Did Miss Josephine actually pine away of a broken heart when she learned her handsome lover had been killed? Such questions today will likely never be answered. Perhaps Dr. Bryce summed it up best in 1921, when, after talking to the hermit, he wrote: "This was a most unsatisfactory story that left me in the dark as to the identity of these people, but it did assure me that within the walls of that old building, still standing, there had been scenes of love and sorrow, mystery and death — secretly locked forever in the graves of these actors long gone."

THE
MAD CARPENTER
OF COCATAMOTH

"It is hardly possible to conceive the extremity of my terror."
— The Narrative of Arthur Gordon Pym

The small headline in Richmond *Enquirer* on Sunday, September 27, 1874, said cryptically: "The Henrico Ghost: A Spectre Carpenter Running His Saw." The brief article beneath it described an extraordinary mystery that has remained unsolved for well over 100 years.

It occurred at the old Cocatamoth estate, about two and a half miles "below" the city on the long-extinct Osborne turnpike. The house was an old fashioned two-story framed building which, in that day, commanded a beautiful view of the James River. It was formerly known as the Tatum residence, bore a "splendid reputation," and was the scene of "many a hospitable gathering."

All of that changed abruptly shortly after J. W. Southard, collector of Varina township, and a "gentleman of good standing," moved into the house with his family. Specifically, the date was Wednesday, September 23, 1874. On that night "commenced manifestations upon the premises which are beyond the ken of any man, and which, to say the least, are passing strange."

Southard, who slept on the ground floor, was awakened early that evening by a noise of what he described as "the drawing of lines on the under side of the floor of his chamber with some blunt instrument." This was followed by the unmistakable sounds of sawing and blows of a hammer and other noises "similar to those made in using various carpenters' tools."

Southard got up and investigated, but could find no source for the disturbance. The next night he heard the same sounds, but again could find nothing. In fact, as soon as he got out of bed, the noise stopped. He walked around the house and then stood outside in the dark for some time, but heard only the natural sounds of nightfall. Maddeningly, as soon as he returned to bed, the phantom carpenter began banging away again and continued until about two in the morning.

When the sawing and hammering began again on Friday, the third successive night, Southard decided he had had enough and was going to get to the bottom of things once and for all. By this time his wife, terrified, said she was leaving to visit relatives in the country until things cleared up.

Working like a man possessed, Southard tore up the floor boards of his chamber, but there was nothing there. He then loaded his double-barreled shotgun, took extra shells, grabbed a knife and a light. He went outside, placed the knife in his teeth, pirate-style, and crawled as far under the house as he could go. He then fired both barrels in the direction of where the noises seemed to be coming from.

Satisfied that he had done all he could, and that if the noises were being made by any mortal being he had silenced the source for good, he retired to bed. No sooner had he turned down the lamp and pulled up his covers, when the hammering and sawing began anew and continued through the night.

Curiously, it was noted that Southard had two "vicious" dogs that slept under the house. Not once during all the activity did they stir, except when he blasted his shotgun.

Southard was described in the article as an "ex-Confederate soldier, and a man who is afraid of nothing, and not the person to make a statement of this character unless it was true." In fact, he offered to take anyone to his place "who doubted his experience with the ghost," and said he was determined to resolve the dilemma if possible.

There is no record of what happened after that — of whether he ever did find out the cause, or whether the incessant nocturnal work of a persistent spirit carpenter eventually drove him and his family from the house.

GHOSTLY TALES AT GRAVESIDE

"By way of amusement, I felt my way among the numerous coffins ranged in order around. I lifted them down, one by one, and breaking open their lids, busied myself in speculations about the mortality within."

— *Loss of Breath*

One gets an eerie sensation while driving through the Cherry Street entrance of Hollywood Cemetary in Richmond. That is because of the caretaker's place which is just off to the right as you go through the gates. If ever a structure *looked* the part of a haunted house, this is it. Even the old edifice Alfred Hitchcock found for his classic horror film, "Psycho," appeared cheerier. And when moonlight splashes across the two-story wooden-framed caretaker's house, it takes a strong will to keep one's imagination from turning into a fantasy chamber of horrors, replete with all sorts of ghouls and ghostly things. Of course, the backdrop to the house — the endless array of graves and tombstones, the rustling of leaves, and the dancing of darkened shadows across headstones and crypts — merely adds to the atmospheric effect. Dare you proceed?

Yes, because Hollywood is one of the most beautiful resting grounds for the dead in the country — and certainly one of the most fascinating. Its gently sloping hills afford picturesque views throughout, and from strategic vantage points, spectacular vistas of the James River rapids and of the city of Richmond are afforded.

Were it not a sanctuary for loved ones who have passed away, it would make a marvelous picnic area. In fact, in olden days such was the custom, when family members faithfully trekked here on Sunday afternoons following church to be near departed relatives and friends. They made a day of it then, long before anyone dreamed of television or the National Football League.

Hollywood Cemetary was founded in 1847. It is said that a delegation of Richmonders drew their plans after viewing other well known burial sites in the country. And it was a shrewd band of businessmen who ran the cemetary. Recognizing the appeal of star attraction, they sought early on to have some national luminaries reinterred here. And they were successful.

The body of Virginian James Monroe, fifth President of the United States, was brought down from New York. John Tyler, the tenth President, lies in rest here rather than at his ancestral home at Sherwood Forest. And, in a magnificent coup, the widow of Jefferson Davis, President of the Confederate States of America, was talked into having her husband's body transferred to Hollywood from New Orleans. He came by train, and thousands of admirers in Southern states littered the tracks with magnolia pedals. Here, too, is the tomb of the gallant Confederate General J. E. B. Stuart, and scores of other historic VIPs, as well as many of Richmond's most distinguished citizens. One could spend days walking among the stones, reminiscing about the grandeur days of the South and the stately gentlemen, now here, who once led it.

Hollywood has its share of curiosities, folklore and legends, also. At the foot of Jefferson Davis' tombstone, for instance, is a much smaller grave site. This is where young Joe Davis, son of the Confederate President, lies. He was but five years old when he fell off the balcony at the White House of the Confederacy in Richmond and was killed. Davis, tragically, was to lose all four of his sons before they reached manhood, but little Joe's loss hit him especially hard.

It was 1864, and things were going bad for the South. When Davis learned of his son's death, candles were lit in every window of the Southern White House, and residents recalled that their leader paced from room to room, hands clasped behind his back and head bowed, all through the night. Now they are together in peace.

Oh yes, there are, too, a couple of ghostly legends in Hollywood. More aptly, they are tales that have been spun and respun down through the years, and while actual verification of their authenticity is nigh impossible, they never-theless, deserve some space in the lore of Richmond.

One concerns the great granite pyramid in the cemetary. There are 18,000 Civil War veterans buried here, 11,000 of them unknown soldiers. Many were brought here from the battle of Gettysburg, and were interred enmasse at the site of the pyramid. There are some who swear that they have heard soft moans from these fallen warriors on nights when a full moon has shone. Perhaps those from plantations and farms far away will be forever restless.

The other story involves the statue of a cast iron dog, which stands almost in the shadow of the pyramid. This dog once, in the 19th century, stood in front of a store on Broad Street. And every day, a little girl would come by the store and pet the dog and talk to it soothingly. She loved it as if it were real. Then one day the little girl didn't come by anymore. She died in an epidemic in 1892. They buried her at Hollywood, and because she had such an affection for the cast iron dog, it was placed at her grave site.

There, some will tell you, it stands guard over her to this day, its iron jaws set to chase away any intruders who might bring harm to its little friend.

Interestingly, not far away is the tomb of famous Richmond writer Ellen Glasgow. When she died her will stipulated that her two pet dogs who had preceded her in death, be dug up from the backyard of her house and be buried with her. And there are those who say these dogs can be heard on occasion scampering about late at night.

And so maybe a case can be made that the sounds heard at Hollywood in the wee hours of the morning may not be just the rustling of leaves, the whistling of the wind, and the gentle rush of the rapids. Could they also include the moans of grievously wounded Civil War veterans, and the whines of canines, both real and artificial — each with a mission still to accomplish?

BIZARRE
HAPPENINGS
AT BERKELEY

*"There are few persons, even among the calmest thinkers, who have
not occasionally been startled into a vague yet thrilling half-credence
in the supernatural..."*

— The Mystery of Marie Roget

But for an ironic quirk of fate, the U.S. may have lost two
future presidents and one signer of the Declaration of Independence, and thus the course of American history might
have been dramatically altered — all in the flash of a single
lightning bolt. And therein lies a tale of interest, intrigue and
psychic phenomena that remains unexplained to this day.

It happened on a dark rainy night in 1744. As the storm
gathered fury sweeping up the James River, Benjamin Harrison, IV, master of Berkeley Plantation in Charles City
County, halfway between Richmond and Williamsburg,
dashed through the house closing windows and locking
shutters. In an upstairs bedroom overlooking the river, he
apparently had trouble with a particular window which
seemed to be stuck. He called for help, and two of his daughters, one carrying his infant son, Benjamin Harrison, V, came
to his aid.

As they stood silhouetted in the window, a terrific flash of
lightning struck them, killing all but the infant instantly.
Luckily, there was a doctor in the mansion, a dinner guest. As
was the medical custom in that day, he "bled" the baby, and

Benjamin Harrison, V, survived. Perhaps he would have anyway, but that is what happened. This Harrison, in turn, grew to become a leader of the American Colonies, signed the Declaration of Independence, and sired William Henry Harrison, who distinguished himself as an Indian fighter, earning the name "Tippecanoe," and later was elected ninth President of the United States. His grandson, another Benjamin Harrison, became 23rd President of the United States.

It is said that the ghosts of Benjamin Harrison, IV, and at least one of his daughters have never left Berkeley; that their "presence," in the form of peculiar manifestations, is still regularly felt by the residents, staff members and even visitors to the plantation. More on this later.

First, it is noteworthy to consider the rich historical lore that surrounds Berkeley, which has been described as the finest mansion among the many that dot historic Route 5 linking Richmond and Williamsburg. In fact, there is so much history and color here, it is difficult to know where to begin.

The plantation land itself was part of a grant made in 1619 by King James I to the Berkeley Company and was designated "Berkeley Hundred." There is a controversy surrounding the arrival of the first settlers to this area. In contrast to what many history books report, Virginians are adamant in believing that the first actual observance of Thanksgiving was, in fact, held at Berkeley in 1619, two years before the Pilgrims celebrated in New England.

According to Dr. Samuel E. Burr, Jr., a retired university history professor, Captain John Woodlief left Bristol, England on September 16, 1619, and reached Berkeley Plantation early in December. "On December 4, 1619," says Dr. Burr, "the crew held a Thanksgiving observance. Although many of their number had died during their first year in America, there had been a bountiful harvest, and it seemed right to give thanks for this to a merciful God.

"These English settlers were joined by about 90 American Indians, led by their Chief Massasoit," notes Dr. Burr. "There were religious services — also military drills, games of skill, singing and sumptuous feasts." He says the menu consisted of turkeys, venison, bear meat, greens, herbs, ducks, geese, shellfish, eels, codfish, flounder, wild fruit and berries and a variety of wines and "home brew." He adds that cranberries and pumpkin pies were not added until years later.

It is likely such services, as an annual event, did not last long, however, for it was at Berkeley, on Good Friday, 1622, that a band of marauding Indians stormed the fragile settlement and killed nine people. For years afterward, the 8,000 or so acres of Berkeley Hundred were abandoned.

The site was not reclaimed until 1636. It eventually became the property of John Bland, a merchant of London. His son, Giles Bland, was a favored lieutenant of the rebellion leader, Nathanial Bacon, and when Bacon's insurrection collapsed in 1676, Bland was ordered hanged by, coincidentally, Governor Sir William Berkeley.

The property then came into the possession of Benjamin Harrison III, whose ancestors were from Wakefield. His son, Benjamin IV, built the Georgian style, three-story brick mansion in 1726.

Incidentally, in addition to claiming the first official Thanksgiving, Berkeley also is listed as being the site of the first commercial shipyard, and, in 1621, of having the first bourbon whiskey distilled there. Further distinctions include the fact that every United States President from George Washington through James Buchanan (the 15th) was entertained by the gracious hospitality of the plantation's hosts. Washington, a close friend of Benjamin Harrison, V, often visited.

Both William Henry Harrison, and Benjamin Harrison were born at Berkeley, sharing this singular honor as the ancestral home of two U.S. presidents with only the Adams House in Massachusetts.

There are dubious glories associated with the plantation, too. It was ransacked during the Revolutionary War by Benedict Arnold. During the early years of the Civil War, General McClelland used the house as headquarters for his Army of the Potomac as he battled with Robert E. Lee in his attempts to march on Richmond. Lincoln visited his general there, and at one time there were as many as 140,000 Union troops in the area. It is said the cellar once was used as a prison for Confederate soldiers.

Today, visitors can see Civil War bullets with teethmarks in them where soldiers bit while being operated on. The house was converted to a hospital. And, it was at Berkeley, in July 1862, that Union General Daniel Butterfield composed the classic military strains of "Taps."

It was also during the Civil War that a 14-year-old drummer boy first saw Berkeley. His name was John Jamieson. In the latter years of the war, the house was abused badly, at one point being turned into an animal barn. It lay in disrepair for decades. Jamieson subsequently became a successful engineer, and, 50 years after he had first been there, came back to buy the ruined plantation. His son, Malcolm "Mac" Jamieson moved to Berkeley in 1930, and he and his wife, Grace, have devoted their lives to restoring the place to its original grandeur.

Thus, today, Berkeley is a lovely place to visit. From the front of the house, five terraces, dug during the Revolutionary War, lead to the James River. Boxwood gardens flank the path, which meets with a ladies winter garden of roses and other flowers. Inside, the restored rooms are furnished with Queen Anne secretaries, English Hepplewhite clocks, a 1725 gentleman's chest, and a 1690 William and Mary chest from Scotland, in addition to fine paintings and portraits. The house is open to the public and expert guides retell its rich history daily.

Ah, but what of the ghosts?

Mac Jamieson says one of the most common manifestations is that the balky bedroom window, where Benjamin Harrison IV, and his daughters stood when they were struck by lightning, periodically slams shut by itself, as if closed by spiritual hands.

"For no apparent reason that window sometimes will close by itself," Jamieson says. "I was in the room one day and was telling a friend about the legend, when the window began to come down while we were looking at it. Now," he laughs, "everybody accuses me of having a button that I push to make the window close, which I haven't, of course."

Others have reported sighting the apparition of a young girl with an infant in her arms at the window late at night. Investigations have revealed no one upstairs at the time.

Mac also tells of the legend of the "ghost in the bottom." He says there is a dip in the road leading into the mansion, and for centuries it has been believed to be haunted by a young child who cries at night. Jamieson is skeptical of this story, however. "Personally, I think it probably was an owl, but the plantation owners didn't discourage the story because it tended to keep the slaves in their quarters at night rather than out partying. The owners felt this kept the slaves fresh for a day's work the next morning so they let the tale perpetuate itself."

There is no logical explanation, however, for the plight of a poor photographer who once visited the plantation. First, he took still pictures. One was of the portrait of Mrs. Jamieson's great grandmother, Elizabeth Burford, in the south parlor. But when he got his film developed, the picture was of another person entirely. He accused the staff of shifting the portraits, but no one had moved anything. Then, he rented a television camera and when he set up in the house to shoot film for a proposed documentary, the camera wouldn't work. When he took it back to the camera shop it worked perfectly. Was some spirit guarding the privacy of the house?

Tour guide Vickey Hoover has had a number of experiences with the "presence" in the house, although she is not in the least afraid of it. She feels it is the ghost of Benjamin Harrison. "He just has ways of letting us know he's around at times," she says. She wasn't a believer when she first joined the staff about five years ago, but she soon changed her mind.

"I guess he thought I was being disrespectful and he wanted to show me," she recalls. "Anyway, I was standing in the front hall beside the linen press when the door of it burst open and hit me in the shoulder." This has happened to her three or four times since. "Once I was explaining the phenomenon to a group of tourists, and the door swung open again. I had to tell them I wasn't pressing any secret lever hidden under the carpet." Another time while she stood by the large piece of furniture the door opened and began swinging back and forth. More recently, she returned after two months off on maternity leave. "I kidded with the other hostesses that Benjamin must not know I'm back, one day as I stood in front of the press. Almost as if on signal, I heard three knocks, turned, and saw the door swing open."

Both Vickey and Jennifer Hess also have heard mysterious rattles from time to time. "I was in the laundry room one day," Vickey says, "when I heard the sound. It was like a door rattling in the dining room, but no one was there. There is a candleabra in the front parlor and when anyone walks across the floor in there, you can hear the glass in it tinkling. I have heard this more than once, but each time when I checked no one was in the parlor."

Vickey also has heard a baby crying, when there was no infant in the house. "I heard it crying in the basement. I went down to look but saw nothing, and when I went back up to the breakfast room, it stopped altogether. We're really not afraid of him. He just likes to play tricks on everyone."

One day during the summer of 1984, Mrs. Jamieson called from the main house to the tour guides in an adjacent building and wanted to know who was in her attic. "We told her we didn't know of anyone," says Jan Wycoff, "but she was adamant that she heard distinct footsteps up there. She said she knew it wasn't squirrels or anything like that. It definitely was a human being's footsteps. I checked the attic and the door was bolted shut like it always is. Then I went outside to see if any workmen had any ladders against the house and were working around the attic area. I didn't see anyone."

But it is in the Berkeley dining room where most of the psychic phenomena occurs. "We don't even have to tell tourists we have a ghost," says Virginia Anders, tour guide leader. "Many of them say they feel a presence the minute they walk into the dining room. We just smile. There is something there, but we can't explain it." Other guides nod in agreement. "I took a group into the dining room one day," says Jan Wycoff, "and the minute we entered the room a woman told me, 'you have a ghost in here. I can feel it.' "

Most of these manifestations are centered in a fruit bowl on the dining room table. Anders, for example, carefully placed a fresh apple in the bowl one morning, then before she left the room she heard it drop. She turned around and saw the apple sail through the air and go over a Chinese screen. "I got out of there real fast," she says. "I was frightened." Later, she went back. No one else had been in the room, but the apple now rested comfortably in the bowl where she had first placed it.

Such a scary experience has happened to others on the staff. Wycoff says the apples "come out on their own and fall to the floor without hitting the wide table." Once, she adds, an artificial lemon, fixed to a nail in the bowl, came out and rolled across the table on its own. Curiously, most of the fruit movements seem to occur in the winter months of January, February, and March when there are relatively few tourists afoot.

Another time Wycoff came in before the first tour one morning and found peanuts scattered across the table. "Where did they come from and how did they get there?" she asks. She told fellow guide Vickey Hoover about it, asking her to clean up the mess when she went through. Hoover saw her later and inquired, "what peanuts were you talking about. I didn't see any." They had mysteriously vanished.

"I feel the explanation of the fruit bowl in the dining room lies with Benjamin Harrison, IV," says Anders. "Maybe he doesn't like the arrangement at certain times. I don't know what else to think. We know none of us do it."

C H A P T E R 7

WREXHAM HALL'S "LADY IN RED"

"I am dying, yet shall I live."
— *Morella*

A fairly common manifestation of psychic phenomena, as related to the sighting of ghosts, seems to be the appearance of a wispy or wraith-like figure. Most of the time — maybe in as many as 80 to 90 percent of the cases — it is the figure of a woman. There is no explanation as to why this is. Also, the predominant majority of these feminine "figures" seem to be clad in white or gray if they are clad at all. White and spectral apparently go together. There are numerous tales of women wearing white nightgowns, usually long and flowing. Or they have something white covering their hair. Transparent apparitions frequently are white to those who see them.

But there are many gray ghosts, too. There is a more plausible explanation for this. Servants and slaves who worked in the household almost always wore gray. And many of the stories about spirits, especially in the old South, concerned servants. Some were badly treated and came back to haunt those who inflicted the pain and agony to them. Others may have caused, directly or indirectly, some tragedy in the house, and return as if to make up for their own transgressions. They seek forgiveness.

It is rare, therefore, for a ghost to be associated with bright colors. Thus, the saga of the spectre at Wrexham Hall in Chesterfield County is all the more unusual, for it centers around a "Lady in Red."

Located just south of Chesterfield Courthouse on Route 10, Wrexham Hall was built by Archibald Walthall, although there seems to be confusion as to just when he built it. Walthall was a Captain in the Chesterfield Militia during the Revolutionary War and once operated a grist mill in the county which was destroyed by British troops in April 1771. Depending upon the source, it has been written that the house was erected in 1770...in 1800...and in 1830 — take your pick. One report filed by the Virginia Historic Landmarks Commission states: "The fireplace mantels are the outstanding architectural gems in the house. The mantel in the dining room has open flutes and it has been indicated by someone that this dates the house prior to 1780." If you can assume that the "someone" referred to was an expert, then this might be the truest indication of Wrexham Hall's age.

The matter is somewhat further complicated by the fact that, in a sense, the house is really two houses in one. One wing is actually the older wing of another home, called Fruit Hill, which was built about 1750. Wrexham owners some years back had been seeking suitable period replacements for badly deteriorated flooring. They found what they were looking for at Fruit Hill, then an abandoned farm house on Swift Creek off Brander's Bridge Road. The owners of this house weren't interested in selling just the floors, they wanted to sell the whole thing, and that's how part of Fruit Hill came to be part of Wrexham Hall!

When Archibald Walthall died, he left the house and property to his daughters, Polly and Susannah. Susannah later sold much of the property, but stipulated that a certain plot of land containing the family burial ground be left undisturbed. A later owner of Wrexham, however, knocked down the gravestones, and, in time, the location of the burial plot was lost. It is unknown where the site is today, and that, speculate some, is the reason for the haunting manifestations of the Lady in Red.

She has only been sighted once. That was a number of years ago when Stanley Hague owned the house. He was working in the field across from Wrexham Hall one day when he and his fellow workers noticed a woman dressed in red sitting on the front porch. They all clearly saw her and commented on the color of her dress.

When Hague returned home after the day's work, he asked his wife why her mother, who lived with the couple, had been sitting on the porch all dressed up in red. She looked surprised, and answered that her mother had been in Richmond all day. No explanation was ever found for the vision.

But while the lady has not been seen again, she has made her presence known at Wrexham Hall on a regular basis down through the years. Judge Ernest P. Gates and his wife, Gee Gee, lived in the house for the past several years, and Gee Gee has reported numerous examples of common psychic phenomena. These have usually taken the form of footsteps on the stairs and rocking chairs which rock in the night.

"Lots of times it sounds like someone walking up the steps," she says. "Guests have reported hearing a rocking chair rock at night and they say they feel a presence in the house." People left alone in the house swear they weren't alone; that something or someone was in the room with them. In each instance, Gee Gee or the guest searched the house thoroughly, but found nothing. "I've gotten so used to it that I'm not afraid at all," Gee Gee says. Nevertheless, when she is home alone she often keeps two television sets going so she won't hear the noises.

Shortly after the Gates moved into the house in 1979, their daughter, Gini, heard voices in the hallway near the steps outside her bedroom. She had been decorating her room at the time and she distinctly remembers hearing a woman say, "Oh, I like what she's done — it's beautiful. I like everything she's done." Curious, Gini went into the hall to see where the voices were coming from. Finding no one there, she scoured the entire house, but she was alone.

One day a family friend paid the Gates a visit, and when she was told about the ghost, she scoffed. She said such talk was utter nonsense and she would never believe in the existence of spirits. They were in the main sitting room, where a full bookcase runs floor to ceiling. Before the woman had finished speaking, a book "flew off its shelf" and nearly struck her.

Other occurrences have included family articles that disappear and later reappear; doors that open and close unexpectedly; and occasional inexplicable cold gusts of air that burst through rooms suddenly.

Who is this mysterious lady, why does she haunt Wrexham Hall, and why is she dressed in red? The Gates have not been able to determine the answers to any of these questions. The judge, though, has offered a speculative view that is not inconsistent with other households which have experienced similar phenomena. He says that it could be the spectre of Susannah Walthall, who has remained at Wrexham all these years still searching for her long-lost family graveyard.

DARK DEEDS AT DODSON TAVERN

"My breast heaved, my knees tottered, my whole spirit became possessed with an objectless yet intolerable horror."
— William Wilson

Petersburg has had its share of ghosts over the years. There was, for example, the rather bizarre episode of a very active poltergeist who resided at a minister's house, since torn down, that was located next to the First Baptist Church on Harrison Street. This noisy spirit apparently threw things around the house in fits of rage, so much so, in fact, that over a period of time, shortly after the end of World War II, he or it attracted large crowds of witnesses. One reporter, upon investigating the story, was hit in the head by a flying book, and the resulting publicity in local papers even brought a visit from the late Dr. J. B. Rhyne of Duke University, one of the world's leading authorities on psychic phenomena.

In fact, stories of haunted houses in Petersburg apparently were so prevalent at one time in the mid-19th century that one man changed the plans of his new house so as not to accommodate them. There is an unusual feature about Trapezium Mansion; there are no right angles in the house. That is because when it was built, a slave is said to have convinced owner Charles O'Hara that right angles encouraged ghosts and gremlins. It must have worked because there have been no reported instances of psychic phenomena there.

There have been at nearby Dodson's Tavern, however, located at 311 High Street. One of the oldest houses in the area, it was built in 1753 by John Dodson, and has had a number of illustrious guests during its history. British soldiers lodged there during the Revolutionary War. Lafayette stayed at the tavern while on a tour after the war, and Aaron Burr stopped over while traveling south in 1804 after killing Alexander Hamilton in a duel.

Robert E. Lee lived up the street from the tavern for a time during the Civil War and dined there on occasion. He is said to have written several letters to young Margaret Jane Dodson who lived at the house. She later married George W. Peagram, and it was their son, Col. John Cargill Peagram about whom stories of strange happenings swirl.

Col. Peagram was the last in a long line of Dodsons to live in the tavern. He died in August 1972 at the age of 91. He had originally specified in his will that the house be destroyed when he died so that it would not fall into disrepair. But several friends convinced him instead to bequeath it to the city of Petersburg to assure its preservation.

This was done, and the city immediately made plans to provide security for the house until it could be opened to the public as a historical landmark. One of the first things done was to install a modern burglar alarm system.

"That's when the funny things started to occur," says Worthington Romaine, Col. Peagram's cousin. Romaine had been willed some of the Colonel's personal belongings and he and his wife went to the Tavern one Saturday morning to sort things out and put them in order.

"I remember I shut off the burglar alarm when I first went in," he says. "We worked almost all day. Then in the afternoon when we were ready to leave, I tried to reactivate the alarm, but it wouldn't work. So we called a repairman from Richmond and he came right over. He traced the wires to the kitchen. There, to his astonishment, he found two wires that had been spliced and twisted together and then taped — had somehow been untwisted. We just scratched our heads and looked at each other. How could two spliced wires, twisted together and taped, come apart?"

But that was just for starters. "There was a C & P telephone man working in the house one day on the ground floor, when books began falling out of book shelves and hitting the floor all around him," Romaine says. "Peagram was a great reader and he had a library of over 4,000 volumes in the house. But these books came from the second floor! I know because my daughter was there and saw one of them hit the floor. They seemed to float out of the shelves and drift down to where the telephone man was working.

"Then another curious incident happened to the same man," Romaine continues. "He looked in his tool box and found a piece of wood in it that hadn't been there before. It was a strip of mahogany. He looked around to see where it might have come from. When he got upstairs to the Colonel's bedroom, he noticed a large mahogany wardrobe against the wall. It had a piece missing from the corner and this strip fit it perfectly. The telephone man fit it back into place and went back downstairs. A little later he looked in his tool box and there was the strip of wood again! No one else was in the house at the time, least of all upstairs. This so unnerved the man that he rushed out of the house and told his supervisor he wouldn't go back inside to work unless the supervisor came with him."

Others experienced similar happenings. According to one published report, a workman came running out of the house one day and said he would never go back in. He said a book had hit him in the chest while he was standing alone in a room. Later, he relented and went back in, only when accompanied by several city policemen. He told one of the officers to "watch me like a hawk. You'll see something."

Just then a penny — one of three that had been resting on a ledge — "jumped" off and hit the floor beside the workman. Next a book tumbled from a shelf near him and fell to the floor. This caused a stir of conversation and as they were discussing these strange events, they heard a "plop" in the bathroom down the hall. There they found a book on the floor next to the commode. There had been no books in the room before.

One who was in the house during this period was Robert Swander, then Petersburg's assistant city manager. "It was a little bit eerie," he recalled. "There were some things that were unexplainable. I never saw the ghost, but there were things moving around. Window shades were flapping and they weren't near open or broken windows or heat ducts. As a skeptic, I looked for those things."

Reportedly, Peagram's daughter died in one of the beds in the house. Swander said once some people present were using candles or butane lighters for illumination, but "when we got near the bed where the girl died, the flames slowly got shorter until they went out. There was never any flicker as if they had been blown out. They just got smaller until they went out. Those same candles had burned downstairs for 30 minutes." Swander added that although the heat was on in the house, it was "ice cold" in the room. "We were in the house from 9:30 p.m. until midnight and the room never heated. You could feel the heat coming out of the heat duct in the room, but when you opened the door to the room there was a burst of cold air."

Oddly, after about a two month period, the poltergeist-like manifestations ceased altogether. The house was sold at public auction by the city to Mr. and Mrs. Robert W. Cabaniss of Hanover in October 1975. They restored the tavern and later sold it to Mr. and Mrs. Grey Lewis of Alexandria. Neither couple ever told of witnessing anything out of the ordinary.

Whatever it was that had upset the ghost of Col. Peagram apparently had been settled after he had made his displeasures known.

THE "MODERN" SPIRIT OF MANCHESTER

"While I nodded, nearly napping, suddenly there came a tapping, As of someone gently rapping, rapping at my chamber door."
— The Raven

In almost every case — in Richmond and elsewhere — ghosts are associated with old houses. Most date to the early 19th century, the 18th century or even earlier, and often the spectral phenomena is linked to one of the first residents of a particular structure. Twentieth century hauntings are unusual. Experts really have not said much about why this is true. Of course, it is reasonable to assume that some tales, perhaps launched in whimsy generations ago, have been colored and added to over the years. If they are told and retold enough times they tend to build an air of credibility. There also seem to be fewer ghosts today than there were in the past.

It is therefore curious at least that the former Manchester Rescue Squad headquarters in Henrico County was haunted, for the building is but 30 years old. Yet, haunted it was, according to a number of the squad members who experienced persistent "visitations" from some unknown source.

One who remembers it well is Harry Boyd, a former county patrolman who has since moved to Virginia Beach. He described the occurrences as "extraordinary auditory phenomena. We never had any visual manifestations," he says. No one ever saw anything." But there were sounds aplenty. Usually, the noises began after the crew had gone to bed. It sounded like somebody coming in through the front door. You could hear the door opening and closing. Then you heard footsteps shuffling back through the bay area where the units were parked. It sounded like all the doors on the units opening and closing in succession."

Boyd said each time anyone got up to investigate, they found nothing. "At first, we thought maybe it was the building settling, or the furnace making noises." But that didn't explain the continuation of sounds in the springtime, when both the furnace and the air conditioner were not in use. Boyd, who has a degree in police science from Virginia Commonwealth University, described himself as a "natural skeptic. However, I'm convinced things do happen that I just can't explain.

"One night in the kitchen, for example, it sounded like all the dishes had been shattered and the silverware dumped out on the floor. But when we rushed in to check, we found nothing out of place." Another time, a rookie scoffed at the ghostly din, daring the spirit to make itself known.

"Later that night," says Boyd, "I thought the walls were going to cave in. It sounded like someone was inside the walls, beating them in with a sledge hammer. It wasn't like a flat rapping. It was more like thunder booming off the ceiling and the walls of the men's bunk room." And, he declares it wasn't anyone's idea of a practical joke, because the banging, which started at about 11 p.m., didn't let up until five the next morning.

At one time Boyd even tape recorded some of the incidents. On one he taped 20 minutes of rhythmic rapping noises, and on another a sound similar to crystal glasses clinking as if in a toast. So regular were the noisy visits, that the crew members nicknamed the ghost "Clarence."

And while Clarence never committed any violent acts, he nevertheless created his share of havoc at the station. Several volunteers, perhaps more superstitious than others, quit the force in fear. It got so bad at one time that some of the dispatchers refused to sit by themselves at night. One, Peggy Schoosmidt, ran into the men's bunk room late one evening when the noises got so loud she became too frightened to stay in the dispatch area.

Squad volunteer Steve Grissom said, "I definitely believe there was a possibility that there was some sort of energy at work there, and Jon Fielder added that he was certain there was something "unusual" in the building at 3213 Broad Rock Road. "Sometimes the noise would almost lift you out of bed," he said. "I wish I could explain it."

Veteran squad member Will Braithwaite offered a possible explanation for Clarence. "There were spirits out there," he noted. "If you die in the back of an ambulance, there's bound to be spirits hanging around."

One expert who lends agreement to Braithwaite's theory is Dr. Glenn Hawkes, a psychologist and parapsychology instructor at Virginia Commonwealth University. "In any place where there have been strong emotional or violent events," he said, "there often appears to be some kind of an effect that persists for long periods of time, unless the building is torn down or removed."

It sounds plausible, but if that is true, how does one explain this interesting footnote to the case of Clarence and the Manchester Rescue Squad? The squad moved to a new location about two years ago. No footsteps, rappings, bangings or any other noises out of the ordinary have been heard since!

THE RETURN OF ELLEN GLASGOW

"Ye who read are still among the living; but I who write shall have long since gone my way into the region of shadows."
— *Shadow* — A Parable

The sound is usually heard late at night. It is a distinct sound — the soft clacking of keys on an old manual typewriter. And it is heard only in one place in the house — in the northwest room on the second floor. That was her den, where she did all her work.

A number of people have heard the midnight typing over the years. Others have claimed that people's imaginations have run wild; that these tapping sounds can be rationally explained. It is, they say, the bursting of seed pods from magnolia trees hitting against the windows. But this does not explain the fact that each time anyone has investigated the source of the sound by opening the door to this particular upstairs room, the tapping mysteriously ceased, only to begin anew once the door was shut again.

Among those who have heard it, some are convinced it can be only one thing — the ghost of famed Richmond novelist Ellen Glasgow — back to complete the novel she left unfinished when she died November 21, 1945, at her long-time home at One West Main Street.

Ellen Glasgow has been described as among the most significant of this nation's 20th century novelists. She wrote 19 novels, all but one set in Virginia. Together, they comprise a social history of the state from 1850 through the author's lifetime. Miss Glasgow won the Pulitzer prize for the best novel of 1941 — "In This Our Life." Critics have said her works have a scope, wit and realism which give them enduring interest, and which made them an influence on the development of American letters. The theme which unified her work was the survival of essential values in the face of adversity, pretension and change.

The critic J. Donald Adams once wrote of her: "I rank her among the best we Americans have produced. In one respect she stands preeminent. She is the wittiest novelist in our history, bar none, and one of the best stylists."

Ellen Glasgow was born in Richmond in 1873. In 1888 her family moved to the residence at One West Main Street, which came to be known as "The Glasgow House." It is a Greek Revival house which was built in 1841 by David M. Branch, a tobacconist. It was purchased in 1846 by Isaac Davenport, one of Richmond's industrial pioneers. He helped build the Franklin Manufacturing Company, the first of the great paper mills of Richmond. His daughter inherited the house when he died, and it was she who sold it to the Glasgows.

Constructed of lightly scored stucco over brick, the house incorporates two stories over a full basement. The deck-on-hip roof is pierced by four interior chimneys, and the edge of the roof is skirted by a molded cornice with bead and reel and dentil courses. The facade is composed of three bays on the main mass and a one bay wing recessed on the east side. The centrally located Doric portico combines a simple molded cornice with a plain frieze and architrave, supported by fluted Greek Doric columns. The front yard is enclosed by a cast iron fence with an open crest work lower border and fluted posts topped with pineapples.

The interior of Glasgow House displays the elegance of Greek Revival detail. The most positive trace of Miss Glasgow's former presence is the unusual wall paper in her second floor study. Imported from England, the paper was so highly prized by the author that she went so far as to insure its preservation in her will. The paper depicts, in an almost Impressionistic manner, the red tile roofed houses of the Mediterranean.

After Miss Glasgow died in 1945, her brother, Archer Glasgow, presented the house to the Virginia Historical Society. Two years later the Association for the Preservation of Virginia Antiquities purchased the house with money collected from friends and relatives who gave generously to preserve it as a landmark to the noted writer. The University Center of Virginia occupied the house from 1947 to 1971, and it was during this period that a number of people saw, heard and felt the presence of what they believed to be Ellen Glasgow's ghost.

One who felt this was Roy Carter, an assistant professor of dramatic art at Virginia Commonwealth University. While a student at Richmond Professional Institute, he lived in the house for awhile, and later, in 1954, returned for a visit.

"I was downstairs with a friend when a compulsion suddenly came over me to get the key and go up to Miss Glasgow's old office," he recalls. "I went upstairs, opened the door, and from that point until my friend called to me about 30 minutes later, I don't remember anything about the room itself. It was almost as though I had gone to sleep. In that time a story was revealed to me concerning Miss Glasgow and another Richmond literary figure. I later checked it, and though I had known nothing about it before, found the story to be true," Carter says.

"When my friend called, I was acutely aware of a clock ticking loudly — but there was no clock in the room. I felt very close to 'Miss Ellen' without knowing why. I felt her presence. I didn't hear any voices, nor did I hear or see anything else. But I perceived *something.*"

Another who has experienced the ghostly manifestations at Glasgow House is Dr. W. Donald Rhinesmith, formerly head of the University Center, and now associated with the state library. He lived in the house for a period, slept in Miss Glasgow's old bedroom, and used her study for a living room.

"I believe in ghosts, but not as anything unfriendly or malignant that can do you harm," he said in a newspaper interview some years ago. "I am convinced that there is a spirit in this house on occasion. I don't know that it stays here all the time. There's something walking around at night, methodically walking, a rather heavy tread as if a troubled spirit is walking in her study, and one night. . .in my bedroom I definitely felt a presence.

"It was about 12 o'clock at night," Dr. Rhinesmith says, "and I had just gone to bed when I heard footsteps coming around the four poster bed, walking toward the window, where I heard a foot stamp. I immediately got up and turned on the lights. "Why," he asks, "would she stamp her foot?" Then he answers, "Well, there used to be handsome Greek Revival houses across Foushee Street. Now there's an ugly parking lot.

"There's a push button buzzer on the wall near the bathroom that Miss Glasgow used to ring for the servants. It's been disconnected for years, but sometimes it rings," he adds. Oddly, none of these happenings aroused the interest of Dr. Rhinesmith's two dogs, who lived in the house with him. Dogs generally can sense anything supernatural and often react to it violently, with snarls, barking and raised hair on their backs. These dogs just slept peacefully. He explained this by noting that Miss Glasgow was a great lover of dogs throughout her life and gave a tremendous amount of support to the SPCA. Two of her pet dogs, in fact, were dug up from their backyard graves and reburied near her gravesite in Hollywood Cemetary, which is adjacent to that of Confederate General J. E. B. Stuart.

Michael Christopher, former owner of the Barn Dinner Theatre, was a student in 1965 when he lived in the basement of Glasgow house. On Thanksgiving evening of that year he returned to the empty house and saw a woman facing him on the stairway landing. He looked to the wall on his right at a picture of Miss Glasgow, and when he looked again at the woman facing him, she was gone. The woman's resemblance to the picture was so real that it totally unnerved him. He left the house immediately and would not return, not even for his possessions!

Earlier in the year, Christopher and others heard a typing sound coming from Miss Glasgow's study. The noise stopped, he said, when the door was opened, and it began again when it was closed. Ruth Norris, who worked in the house once, remembers sensing the "feeling of a benevolent spirit" there. She once heard a woman's voice singing three notes on the musical scale. But when she searched for the source she found no one else there.

A recent call to Dr. Rhinesmith brought his reaffirmation that something ghostly exists in the house, which currently is occupied by the law firm of McCaul, Grigsby, Pearsall, Manning and Davis. "I definitely heard the stamping feet on the floor," Dr. Rhinesmith says, "when no one was there. Others claimed to see a woman on the landing. Most of us just assumed it was Miss Glasgow, but some believed it may have been another woman who lived in the house earlier.

"In fact, in her autobiography, 'The Woman Within,' Miss Glasgow mentions having had a horrible vision on the stairs, so she could have seen the figure, too." Indeed, in this volume she states in one passage that "ghosts were my only companions." She went on: "This is not rhetoric. This is what I thought or felt or imagined, while I stood there, in that empty house, with the few strident noises floating in from the street, and my eyes on the darkness of the garden beyond the thick leaves on the porch. I felt, literally, that I was attacked by fear, as by some unseen malevolent power."

So, the question remains: is the ghost of Glasgow House that of Ellen Glasgow, who endured a number of deep personal tragedies while living there, and who died in her sleep before finishing her last novel? Or is it that of another woman who suffered some unknown sorrow and unpleasantness more than a century ago? Is it possible that there are *two* ethereal beings that co-exist; one who types late at night and rings a disconnected buzzer for ancient servants to answer; the other who appears periodically on the stairway landing, and occasionally is heard singing?

C H A P T E R 1 1

A TRILOGY
OF TERROR
IN GOOCHLAND

"The spirits of the dead who stood
In life before thee are again
In death around thee, and their will
Shall overshadow thee: be still"
— *Spirits of the Dead*

Some of the more colorful ghosts in the area have surfaced over the years in Goochland County, to the west of Richmond. While the majority of spiritual manifestations take the rather mundane forms of rappings, footsteps, wispy apparitions and muffled sobs and cries, Goochland haunts have demonstrated an imaginative flair by comparison. Herewith, for instance, is a trio of tales that have been passed along in the county and were reported upon some years ago in a publication of the Goochland Historical Society. They include, for variety: a disappearing corpse; a huge black dog through which bullets pass without rendering harm; and a headless woman who descends stairs with a seemingly inexhaustible supply of fresh lamps.

* * * * * *

The first concerns a certain Dr. Morriss Barret who lived at a place called Mount Bernard. Just when his experience occurred is unknown, but it likely was in the second half of the

19th century or very early in the 20th, because his mode of transportation was horse and buggy. As it is told, he and his wife were traveling home on a night washed with moonlight after having visited some friends.

As they reached a point known as Black Rock, named for a huge black rock there, about halfway between Mount Bernard and Plynlimmon, Mrs. Barret cried out that there was a man lying in the road. The doctor pulled hard on the reins, but he couldn't stop in time and the buggy wheels bumped over the inert form lying face up on the ground.

The doctor quickly descended from the buggy to tend the man. In the strong moonlight, he gasped in startled recognition. "It is Jim Lewis," he said. "I haven't seen him around here for a long time." Lewis, it seemed, had worked for the doctor on occasion. Then a very mysterious thing happened. As Dr. Barret reached for Lewis, the form of the body "slid out of range and into space." It disappeared before his eyes.

Dumbfounded, Barret told his wife, "I can't understand it at all. That was Jim Lewis lying in the road. I even saw the jagged scar on his left cheek, but when I went back there — he — he just vanished."

The next day a man from the city morgue in Richmond called on the doctor and asked him if he would come view a body in the morgue in hopes of identifying it. As this was not an uncommon request in his profession, Barret went. But when he returned home, he was visibly shaken. "The man in the morgue," he told his wife, "is Jim Lewis. He has been there two weeks! How could he be in the morgue and in the road at the same time?"

Dr. Barret, it may be added, was known as a sober, intelligent professional, not given to fits of fantasy.

* * * * * *

Oldtimers still talk about the big black dog in Goochland County. They say it was the size of a young calf. It roamed about the county and claimed sightings of it were made near the State Farm, at the entrance to Thorncliff and at Chestnut Hill Bottom. He often appeared out of nowhere to trot alongside someone walking, on horseback, or riding a buggy.

Despite its grotesque size and appearance, the dog seemed harmless.

One person who experienced such company was a prominent lawyer named P. A. L. Smith, Sr. He used to walk from his home to the State Farm to get the train to Richmond, and on many evenings when he returned and walked back home in the dark, the big dog joined him.

There was a woman, too, who lived near the State Farm, and she told quite an extraordinary story of the dog. She claimed it entered her house one night by opening the screen door. It then walked over to her old-fashioned ice box, unfastened the door, helped itself to some food, and then, carefully, closed the door and left the house. It should be added that other strange events took place in this particular house. In fact, when it was vacant, people came to "see and hear the windows and doors rock and rattle."

Many people didn't seem inclined to discount the woman's narrative, because there were even more peculiar dog "anecdotes." Some of the local citizens didn't take kindly to having the dog accompany them, and on more than one occasion they shot the beast with their pistols. Eerily, the bullets passed through the dog's body and he kept right on trotting beside them. Needless to say, this abruptly changed their annoyance into raw fright.

* * * * * *

Perhaps the best known ghost in Goochland County, however, resides at Plynlimmon House — a large, rambling frame structure once owned by Judge Isaac Pleasants, a cousin of Governor James Pleasants. No one has ever determined the identity of this spectral semblance, principally because it is headless! But many claimed to have seen "her." The circumstances are always the same. After everyone had retired for the evening, she would appear at the top step of the stairway dressed in a "white wispy sort of gown that billowed out as she walked." She carried a lighted lamp in her hands.

Then she would begin to slowly descend the stairs. About halfway down she suddenly would throw the lamp in the air and hurl her body the remainder of the way, letting out a "blood-curdling scream" as she did. Then she vaporized into thin air before any astonished observers.

This allegedly went on for many years. Some have speculated that it may have been an early resident of the house who tripped on the stairs one evening and was killed in the fall. But no one can offer any explanation as to why she is headless.

One county resident who doubted the story, went out to the house one night when it was vacant to see for himself. He was not disappointed. She appeared, and fell to the floor as usual, making an instant convert of him. More than that, he resolutely swore to anyone who would listen that he found fresh blood on the stairs where she had passed!

A SCENE OF INDESCRIBABLE HORROR

"And Darkness and Decay and the Red Death held illimitable dominion over all."
— *The Masque of Red Death*

It is known throughout Richmond simply as *the* fire.

It occurred the day after Christmas in the year 1811, during James Madison's first term in office as the fourth President of the United States. The site was a theatre on the north side of Broad Street between 12th and College. The occasion was the presentation of a new play, "The Bleeding Nun," a comic-pantomine. The combination of the season, the new play and the appearance of a popular actress drew an audience of 600 persons, "among whom were some of the most distinguished men of Virginia, and a large number of the most cultivated and refined of the citizens of Richmond, male and female." These included Governor George Smith.

In the words of the editor of the Richmond *Enquirer*, who was present: "It was the fullest house of the season...The play went off; the pantomine began; the first act was over; the whole scene was before us, and all around us was mirth and festivity."

It happened just after the start of the second act. Backstage, a young boy was ordered by one of the players to raise a chandelier of open lighted candles. He stated that if he did so the scenery might catch fire. The player then commanded him "in a peremptory manner" to hoist the chandelier.

Here, we pick up the newspaper account: "The boy obeyed and the fire was instantly communicated to the scenery. He gave the alarm in the rear of the stage and requested some of the attendants to cut the cords by which these combustible materials were suspended. The person whose duty it was to perform this business became panic struck and sought his own safety. This unfortunately happened at a time when one of the performers was playing near the orchestra, and the greatest part of the stage, with its horrid danger, was obscured from the audience by a curtain.

"The flames spread with almost the rapidity of lightning, and the fire falling from the ceiling upon the performer was the first notice which the people had of the danger. Even then, many supposed it was part of the play." At this juncture a Mr. Robertson stepped out on the stage, and "in unutterable distress, waved his hand to the ceiling and announced: 'The house is on fire.' "

From here, we follow the scene via the *Enquirer* editor: "The cry of 'fire, fire' passed with electric velocity through the house; everyone flew from their seats to gain the lobbies and stairs. The scene baffles all description. The most heart-piercing cries pervaded the house. 'Save me, save me.' Wives asking for their husbands; females and children shrieking, while the gathering element came rolling on its curling flames and columns of smoke, threatening to devour every human being in the building.

"Many were trod underfoot; several were thrown back from the windows, from which they were struggling to leap. The stairways were immediately blocked up; the throng was so great that many were raised several feet over the heads of the rest; the smoke threatened an instant suffocation. We cannot dwell on this picture. We saw — we felt it — like others, we gave ourselves up for lost; we cannot depict it. Many leaped from the windows of the first story, and were saved; children and females, and men of all descriptions were seen to precipitate themselves on the ground below, with broken legs and thighs, and hideous contusions. . . .

"The fire flew with rapidity almost beyond example. Within ten minutes after it caught, the whole house was wrapped in flames. The colored people in the gallery, most of them, escaped through the stairs cut off from the rest of the house; some have no doubt fallen victims. The pit and boxes had but one common avenue, through which the whole crowd escaped, save those who leaped from the windows. But the scene which ensued it is impossible to paint. Women with dishevelled hair; fathers and mothers shrieking out for their children; husbands for their wives; brothers for their sisters, filled the whole area on the outside of the building. A few who had escaped plunged again into the flames to save some dear object of their regard, and they perished. The Governor perhaps shared this melancholy fate. Others were frantic, and would have rushed to destruction, but for the hand of a friend.

"Every article of the Theatre was consumed, as well as the dwelling house next to it. But what is wealth in comparison to the valuable lives which have gone forever!. . . Heads of families extinguished forever; many and many is the house in which a chasm has been made, that can never be filled up. We cannot dwell upon this picture; but look at the catalogue of the victims, and then conceive the calamity which has fallen upon us. We must drop the pen."

So horrifying was the experience that another editor attending the play that evening was to write: "Alas, gushing tears and unspeakable anguish deprive me of utterance. No tongue can tell — no pen or pencil can describe — the woeful catastrophe. No person, who was not present, can form any idea of the unexampled scene of human distress."

In the midst of all the panic and confusion were individual acts of extraordinary heroism. Governor Smith and a number of other gentlemen lost their lives in attempts to save others. Samuel Mordecai, remembering the night in a book published nearly half a century later, told of the Herculean efforts of a Richmond physician, Dr. James D. McCaw, and a Negro blacksmith named Gilbert Hunt. He wrote: "The doctor had reached a window and broken out the sash, when he and Gilbert recognized each other. He called to Gilbert to stand below and catch those he dropped out. He then seized on the woman nearest to him, and lowering her from the window as far as he could reach, he let her fall. She was caught in Gilbert's arms and conveyed by others to a place of safety. One after another the brave and indefatigable doctor passed to his comrade below, and thus 10 or 12 ladies were saved.

"The doctor, having rescued all within his reach, now sought to save himself. The wall was already tottering. He attempted to leap or drop from the window, but his strong leathern gaiter, an article of sportsman's apparel which he always wore, caught in a hinge or some other iron projection, and he was thus suspended in a most horrid and painful position; he fell at last, but to be lame for life. The muscles and sinews were stretched and torn and lacerated, and his back was seared by the flames, the marks of which he carried to his grave."

In all, 72 people perished in the flames, and countless others were burned. The aftermath was total shock. As was written at the time: "The morning sun rose over the ashes of the Chief Executive of the Commonwealth, and the highest and lowest of the people mingled in an indistinguishable smouldering mass. The holy season for joy and gladness was, to the awe struck community, one of lamentation and of weeping, of deep and bitter sorrow. The state, indeed the whole country, mourned in sincere sympathy with afflicted Richmond."

A day after the fire, on December 27, 1811, the Common Council of Richmond passed the following ordinance: "Whereas, the fire which took place in the theatre on the twenty-sixth instant, has brought upon our city a calamity unknown in the annals of our country, from a similar cause depriving society of many of its most esteemed and valuable members, and inflicting upon its survivors pangs the most poignant and afflicting; and the Common Hall, participating in those feelings, and being desirous of manifesting their respect for the remains which have been preserved from the conflagration, and to sooth and allay as much as in them lies the grief of the friends and relations of the deceased:

"1. Be it therefore ordained by the President and Common Council of the city of Richmond. . .to cause to be collected and deposited in such urns, coffins or other suitable enclosures. . .all the remains of persons who have suffered, which shall not be claimed by the relatives, and cause the same to be removed to the public burying ground, with all proper respect and solemnity, giving to the citizens of Richmond. . .notice of the time of such interment, and providing the necessary refreshments; and they shall have further authority to cause to be erected over such remains such tomb or tombs as they may approve, with such inscriptions as to them may appear best calculated to record the melancholy and afflicting event.

"2. And be it further ordained by the authority of the same, that the constable of the city be authorized to communicate to the citizens, that it is earnestly recommended that they will abstain from all business, keeping their shops, stores, counting houses, and offices shut for 48 hours from the passing of this ordinance.

"3. And be it further ordained that no person or persons shall be permitted for and during the term of four months from the passage hereof to exhibit any public show or spectacle, or open any public dancing assembly within the city, under the penalty of six dollars and sixty-six cents for every hour the same shall be exhibited."

Further, a day of "humiliation and prayer" was set aside, and it was resolved that citizens "wear crepe for a month." On the Sunday following the fire, the remains of those who had died were buried within the area formerly included in the walls of the theatre, and subscriptions were started to raise "an appropriate monument over the tomb."

The original burial site selected apparently had been at St. John's church on Richmond Hill, but for some reason it was changed to the theatre site. The Richmond *Enquirer* of December 31, 1811, described the funeral procession this way: "They moved up Capitol Hill, and at the capitol were joined by the bearers of two large mahogany boxes, in which were enclosed the ashes and relics of the deceased. The mournful procession then moved to the devoted spot, and in the centre of the area where once stood the pit, these precious relics were buried in one common grave . . . The whole scene defies description — a whole city bathed in tears! How awful the transition on this devoted spot! A few days since it was the theatre of joy and merriment, animated by the sounds of music and the hum of a delightful multitude. It is now a funeral pyre! the receptacle of the relics of our friends; and in a short time a monument will stand upon it, to point out where their ashes lay."

That monument is known today as Monumental Church. Its cornerstone was laid just seven months after the fire by a young architect named Robert Mills. He was the only architectural pupil of Thomas Jefferson. The church was completed in 1814, and it is now considered one of the nation's major architectural landmarks. It is the grandest and only remaining example of the five octagonal, domed churches Mills designed. The entire building is ornamented with funereal details and references to the fire. The capitals of two columns feature, as symbols of mourning, upside-down torches, stars and drapes, surrounded by a flame like carving on a pediment.

As an interesting sidelight, among the many worshippers at Monumental Church through the years was a youth named Edgar Allan Poe. In fact, it has been speculated that because the building was actually a tomb rather than a church, it may have had some influence on Poe's brooding style of writing. It is noteworthy, too, that there was an actor-actress couple named Usher who performed at the theatre on the site, possibly even with Poe's actress mother. Poe probably knew of them, which leads to the natural thought that he may have used their name for his classic, "The Fall of the House of Usher." And, there is the irony that Poe's mother, who often acted in the theatre, died about two weeks before the fire.

Today, one can walk down a narrow stairway in the back of Monumental Church to the basement and then across dirt floors to the brick crypt which houses the ashes of those who died in the disaster. It is dark and gloomy, and if ever there were cause for the ghosts of anguished spirits to make themselves known in the form of psychic manifestations, this should be the site. The spirits of burn victims at other buildings have been known to moan, scream and scratch and tear at walls.

But at the darkened crypt in Richmond there is only an ethereal silence. There are no recorded instances of mysterious sights or sounds. It is as if the victims were appeased at the erection of the impressive tomb that shelters them.

Ah, but do not despair! There *is* an authentic ghost story associated with the tragic fire of 1811, although few people have ever heard of it.

More than 100 years were to pass before this extraordinary narrative came to light. It had been orally passed down, generation to generation, in a well known Richmond family, and finally surfaced in 1922, in the form of an unpublished monograph written by a Mrs. Nannie Dunlop Werth. Her work has reposed for years in relative obscurity in the archives of the Virginia Historical Society in Richmond which owns it. It is with the gracious permission of the Society that herewith are selected excerpts from that intriguing document, numbered Mss7:1 G8245:1.

Mrs. Werth was told the story, presumably when she was a young girl, by her grandmother, Mrs. Alexander McRae, whose husband studied law with John Marshall and was prosecuting attorney in the celebrated Aaron Burr trial. She was at the theatre on the night of the fire.

Her mother was Ann Dent Hayes, who "gave to Richmond property which became Leigh Street, and built her own handsome colonial residence, with its mahogany doors and solid silver knobs, on the southeast corner of Leigh Street, known later as the McCance home...Opposite to Mrs. Hayes' home in the centre of the lot extending from 7th to 8th Street on Leigh, was built a most imposing double house, which still remains one of the few landmarks of that period."

This house was owned and occupied by Mr. and Mrs. Patrick Gibson. Mrs. Gibson had adopted as her "ward," a young girl named Nancy Green, daughter of J. W. Green. It was through this girl, who was one day short of her 16th birthday on December 26, 1811, the day of the fire, that a form of psychic phenomena manifested itself.

Mrs. Gibson wanted Nancy to attend the play that evening, but for reasons unknown, Nancy "stoutly refused and declared she did not want to go. Her objections," Mrs. Werth writes, "were finally overcome when her guardian declared that proper respect for her father demanded her presence.

"During the afternoon of the play Mrs. Gibson sent Nancy to Broad Street to make a purchase. Enroute, she passed along

8th Street and crossed the ravine, from whence she said a Ghost called her, chanting: 'Nancy, Nancy, Nancy Green, you'll die before you are sixteen.' "

Mrs. Werth states that her grandmother, Mrs. McRae, was present and heard her recount the threat when she came home. Mrs. McRae thought "a psychological depression had resulted, and caused the child's disclination to go that night to the theatre." She went nevertheless, along with Mrs. Gibson, Mrs. McRae and several others.

Only Mrs. McRae and two others in their party escaped. Reports Mrs. Werth: "Mrs. McRae was pacing up and down the aisle of the second balcony, then the dress circle, suffocating under a heavy burden of smoke, when she was attracted to a nearby window by a burning fragment which fell from the cornice above. She rushed frantically forward seeking fresh air and leaned out. A man's voice cried: 'Jump, I'll catch you.' Knowing it was certain death to disregard the call, she sprang into strong arms and was saved."

Mrs. Gibson died in the inferno, as did young Nancy Green, who, true to prophetic words of the ghost she had encountered that very afternoon, did not live to see her sixteenth birthday!

PREMONITIONS OF DEATH

"In their gray visions they obtain glimpses of eternity, and thrill, in waking, to find they have been upon the verge of the great secret."
— Eleonora

Psychic experiences can take many forms and shapes, and although few of us are possessed with advanced degrees of extrasensory perception, or ESP, most of us at least have had brushes with occurrences we cannot readily explain. Have you ever, for example, gone into a room of a house in which you have never been before and suddenly felt that you knew the room; that somehow, perhaps subconsciously, you *had* been there before?

Premonition is one form of psychic phenomena. Have you ever had the feeling that something was going to happen, and it did, exactly as you perceived? There are countless, well documented incidents of such cases. Many of them seem to involve the dream or nightmare of a person who envisions their loved one dying.

Consider the case of Julia Gardiner Tyler, for instance. The wife of John Tyler, 10th President of the United States, she lived with her husband at the Sherwood Forest Plantation in Charles City County, 35 miles from Richmond. In January 1862, the ex-Chief Executive rode to Richmond to attend a conference. Julia was to join him a week later. However, she had a horrifying nightmare in which she envisioned him dying in a large bed with a headboard of "a great carved eagle with outstretched wings." She was so upset at the vividness of her dream that she went at once to Richmond by carriage. He was found perfectly healthy and scoffed at his wife's dream.

Incredibly, two days later he suffered an attack at the Exchange Hotel and died in a bed that in precise detail matched the one Julia had seen in her dream!

A strikingly similar case involved Colonel Robert Gamble early in the 19th century. (Richmond's Gamble's Hill area is named after him.) He was born in Augusta County, Virginia, and served with distinction in the Revolutionary War, fighting in battles at Princeton, Monmouth and Stony Point. He, in fact, lost his hearing when one of the enemy's cannons discharged just as he reached it.

After the war he married Catharine Grattan, an Irish lass who had migrated to Rockbridge County with her parents. She was described as a woman "of great energy and character," who once rode 30 miles on horseback at night, with her sister's infant on her lap, to warn settlers of an Indian attack.

After living for awhile in Staunton, the Gambles moved, in the 1790s, to Richmond. A prosperous businessman, the Colonel bought a mansion on the outskirts of town designed by the noted architect, Benjamin Labrobe, and lived comfortably "in the enjoyment of elegant hospitality." Such a lifestyle included a large household, servants, a handsome carriage, and a stable full of thoroughbred horses.

Gamble rode into Richmond each day to attend to his various business interests, and returned home each evening. This habitual existence continued for years. That is, until the morning of April 12, 1810. At breakfast, the Colonel noticed his wife seemed depressed. He inquired, and she told him she would very much appreciate it if he didn't go into town that day. Curious, he asked why.

She told him she had dreamed the previous night that if he left the house this day he would never enter it alive again. The Colonel did not take this warning lightly, for his wife seemed to possess what then was known as "second sight." Today, it might be called a psychic sense. Still, being a practical man himself, he dismissed her fears, mounted his favorite horse, and went into the city.

He bought a paper on the way, and as he was riding through the warehouse section of Richmond reading it, chance overtook him. A large bundle of buffalo hides was tossed out of an upper window and landed bang in front of his horse, causing it to rear suddenly. Gamble was thrown to the ground where his head struck a rock. He suffered a brain concussion and died.

His associates gathered and formed a group to accompany his body home and inform Mrs. Gamble. At the Colonel's house they were astonished to find her, dressed in black, seated in the downstairs hall, surrounded by frightened servants.

Before any explanation could be offered by the group of men, Mrs. Gamble spoke: "You see," she told them, "I begged him not to venture into the city today, for I knew if he did he would never return to this house alive." Then she told them of her dream. "That is why," she added, "when he insisted on going, I went upstairs immediately and put on my best black silk dress in order that I would be suitably attired to receive his corpse when it was brought home."

* * * * * *

Another form of premonition concerning the bearing of bad news occurs when a relative or loved one has a vision of a person, often at the precise moment of that person's death. It is as if the spirit of the freshly departed person is trying to communicate to the ones closest to him.

A classic example of this occurred in Richmond in the late 1840s and has been passed down through the generations as legend, although the exact names, dates and addresses of the people involved have been lost in the sands of time.

The story concerns a young officer in the United States Army who was serving in the Mexican War. We are told only that he was a member of a prominent family in the city, and that his first name was James.

His younger brother was awakened from a deep sleep one morning to find the officer standing at the foot of his bed in full uniform. He was surprised to see his older brother, for there had been no word that he was coming home. He asked

him when he had gotten back.

James apparently replied with only this cryptic answer: "Major Smith will see you later and tell you all about it." With that, James turned, walked to the door and passed through into the hall. His brother sprang from the bed and ran into the hall. There was no one there. He then searched the house and garden, but found nothing.

Not long after that, a Major Smith arrived at the house and informed the family of the young officer's death. He had died at precisely the moment his brother had envisioned his image.

THE DISASTER OF DAHLGREN'S RAID

"All in vain; because Death, in approaching him, had stalked with his black shadow before him, and enveloped the victim."
— The Tell-Tale Heart

There was a time, early in 1864, when a siege of the city appeared imminent. Richmonders feared not only that their town would be sacked and burned, but there had been vicious rumors circulating that the hated Yankees intended to publicly execute Jefferson Davis and his entire cabinet. As fear swept through the town, talk of violent retaliation increased. One idea fostered by Southern zealots was to hang the Union prisoners at Belle Isle — all 15,000 of them. Such thoughts were quickly quelled by cooler heads.

Still, for a time Richmond was in some danger, and had a rather ingenious plan hatched by Brigadier General Judson Kilpatrick worked, the Capitol of the Confederacy could have fallen. As it was, Kilpatrick's idea led to a colorful sidebar to the war that came to be known as Dahlgren's Raid. Therein lies a strange and absorbing story complete with the unfortunate hanging of a poor young black, the mutilation of the body of the Raid's leader, and the haunting reoccurrence — to this day — of the ghosts of a Federal officer, and a tortured slave.

Kilpatrick reasoned that with Lee's Army of Northern Virginia off fighting in the wilderness, Richmond was vulnerable to a bold surprise attack. He sold his superiors on a plot where he would lead a detachment of 4,000 troops through the thin Southern lines and openly confront what defenses the city still maintained. The key would be while he drew the major fire, a smaller force of 500 men would sneak in behind the home guard, ford the James River, and free the 15,000 Union prisoners. This, Kilpatrick believed, would break the Confederate spirit, and the city would surrender. Admittedly, it was a gamble, but one daring enough to have the possibility of succeeding.

To lead the smaller raiding party, Kilpatrick, who was only in his mid-twenties, chose a man named Ulric Dahlgren. At 21, he was said to be the youngest colonel in the Northern army. Earlier in the war, the tall and dashing Dahlgren had been severely wounded in a calvary skirmish at Boonsboro, Maryland, and his right leg had to be amputated. After months of convalescence and fitted with a wooden leg, Dahlgren and his 500 men started out.

It was an innovative plan, but one destined to disaster by the elements of reality. Confusion, foul weather and the unerring accuracy of persistent Confederate snipers along the route all took their toll. Dahlgren lost contact with Kilpatrick's larger force and attempts to reestablish communications proved futile. The ultimate irony occurred when a young black, who had told the youthful colonel he knew the best place to cross the river, led the troops to a point where the James, swollen by storms, was both deep and treacherous. Dahlgren thought the black had betrayed him and, probably impetuously, ordered his hanging.

Realizing the mission was lost, Dahlgren ordered his soldiers to retreat. They got separated in the darkness of the woods. About 300 eventually made it back to the Union lines. Dahlgren and the other 200, however, were missing, and it was days before their fate was learned. He had struck off for the northeast and made reasonably good progress, at one point making a spectacular crossing of the Mattapony River. But by now, word of the invasion had spread, and snipers seemed to loom behind every barn and tree.

In the middle of the night a force of Virginia cavalry, reinforced with home guards and rifle-carrying farmers, positioned themselves for an ambush in the forest. Dahlgren, leading his men, pistol in hand, heard men moving in the woods and shouted: "Surrender, you damned Rebels, or I'll shoot you!" His challenge was met with a heavy volley of fire, and he fell dead from his horse, his body riddled with bullets. Chaos reigned and most of his men were either killed or captured. Little mercy was shown since the raiders had set fire to barns, flour mills, railroad buildings and freight cars along the way. They had ravaged farms and stolen what little food they could find.

Some of the hatred was vented on Dahlgren's body. One man cut off his finger to get a ring. Another took his artificial leg as a souvenir, and he was stripped of his watch, other valuables and his clothing. Ingloriously, his body was carted to Richmond in a lidless pine box where it was displayed in a railroad station. Later, after having been interred, the corpse was "dug up and buried again, secretly, and with every indignity, as that of an outlaw."

At one point someone allegedly found papers on Dahlgren's body describing the intent of his raid. They may well have been forged. Still, when the paper's content was exposed in the press, saying that the thousands of Union prisoners were to have been let loose on the city, it conjured up wild visions of rape, plunder and murder. The Richmond *Examiner*, for example, said: "... turning loose some thousands of ruffian prisoners, brutalized to the deepest degree by acquaintance with every horror of war, who have been confined on an island for a year, far from all means of indulging their strong sensual appetites — inviting this pandemonium to work their will on the unarmed citizens, on the women, gentle and simple, of Richmond, and on all their property."

Northern journalists, in turn, decried the mutilation of Dahlgren's body, the hanging of the young black man, and the hunting down of Union soldiers with packs of bloodhounds. The furor rose to such heights that Lee sent General Meade a message asking for an answer to charges of intended barbarity. Meade replied that no one had ordered any cities burned or civilians harmed.

And thus ended Dahlgren's Raid, and, for a time, the threat to Richmond. The two ghostly sidelights to this historic vignette linger on, however. One, which was mentioned in the Sunday magazine section of a Richmond newspaper nearly half a century ago, concerns an "old house on Three Chopt Road owned by Ben Green." It was there that some of Dahlgren's men tried to learn the location of the household silver, which was "known to be extensive," and thought to be buried nearby. When a "faithful" old slave named Burwell refused to disclose the hiding site he was strung up by his thumbs. This house, according to the article, "is known to be haunted." Some believe it is the spirit of Burwell who remained, seeking some form of retribution for the brutal pain he suffered so long ago.

The other legend centers around one of Dahlgren's young officers. He rode his horse into a dense patch of honeysuckle thicket surrounded by trees somewhere on Cary Street Road in an area where an old ice house once stood. He immediately fell, mortally wounded. It has been reported that on calm nights "are frequently heard moans from the luckless victim."

THE GHOST OF GOVERNOR'S MANSION

"I was awakened from a slumber, like the slumber of death, by the pressing of spiritual lips upon my own."

— *Eleonora*

The Governor's Mansion in Richmond, the construction of which commenced in 1813, has seemed to mellow and improve with age, as has its acceptance among Virginians. Today, for example, a Virginia Historic Landmarks Commission report calls it, "one of the state's outstanding examples of Federal style architecture." And a booklet prepared at the direction of Mrs. Mills E. Godwin, Jr., wife of the former governor, describes the mansion thusly: "the solid old house still seems relatively unaffected by the passage of its many gubernatorial generations. Despite renovations, restorations, and re-arrangements, it remains the very essence of Virginia."

Such was not always the case. Certainly, it was, when built, an improvement over the "unpretentious" four room wooden house that stood at the same site housing earlier chief executives. It had fallen into "bad repair" and was torn down to make room for the new building.

Boston architect Alexander Parris was commissioned to draw preliminary plans for the mansion, but the Commissioners of Public Buildings were not satisfied that these properly reflected the "honor and dignity of the state," so they added some embellishments of their own. Whatever it was they did, it apparently didn't please many people.

Not long after it was finished, for instance, a Richmond newspaper stated the building was furnished in a style of inferiority "almost discreditable to Virginia." It further called the mansion's exterior "one of the homeliest dwellings in the city." One later governor's wife was even more sarcastic in her criticism. When she moved in, she said there were only three antiques in the house — "a tin roof, ugly floors, and copper bathtubs." She also noted that the carpets hadn't been taken up for 40 years.

The furniture at one time was in such a rickety state that a visiting chairman of the General Assembly's finance committee — admittedly, he was a rather large man — demolished a gilt chair when he sat down. It splintered beneath his bulk into kindling and so embarrassed him, he tried to hide the remains of the chair in a potted palm.

In time, however, a number of improvements were made to the house. Governor James Barbour, who reportedly was not satisfied with the "stark, rectangular structure," added balustrades along the eaves, and railed in the four Georgian chimneys to form a "captain's walk." Later, porticoes were added to make the north and south entrances "more inviting." Eventually, the tin roof was replaced with slate, and the copper bathtubs with porcelain.

The oval dining room was added by Richmond architect Duncan Lee, moving the outdoor kitchen into the basement, and "throwing open" the two back rooms on the first floor to form the present ballroom. More recently, the north evergreen garden was added, as was, too, a breakfast room, a library and a study. And, through the years the furnishings have been upgraded to the point where, today, the mansion contains a fairly impressive array of Hepplewhites, Sheratons, Chippendales and Duncan Phyfes, along with a fine collection of portraits, paintings, porcelains, figurines and a splendid silver service.

The attitude of the public about the mansion also has evolved through the decades, from one described once in a report as "indifference and sometimes caustic criticism," to respect and affection. This feeling has been presumably shared by some of the notable guests of the house, including five U.S. Presidents, Winston Churchill, King Edward VII, Queen Mother Elizabeth of England, Charles Lindbergh, and Admiral Richard E. Byrd.

Add to this prestigious list the fact that four future U.S. Presidents — Thomas Jefferson, James Monroe, William Henry Harrison, and John Tyler, plus Patrick Henry have all lived at the site, and General Stonewall Jackson's body lay in state in the house in 1863.

It is against all this colorful background that we learn that an intruder, too, has tenanted the Governor's Mansion, in the form of the apparition of a beautiful young lady. She reputedly was first encountered in the early 1890s by none other than Governor Philip W. McKinney himself, surely a credible witness.

He came in one hot August afternoon from the Capitol, took his coat off and washed up in a bathroom, and then entered a bedroom, only to be startled by "a young lady sitting in the window." He quietly and quickly retreated to his wife's room and asked her who her guest was. She replied, "I haven't any guest," whereupon he reentered the bedroom and the lady had vanished. A search of the mansion turned up no clues as to her identity or mission.

There was one other occasion where the mystery woman

was actually seen. According to officer Robert Toms of the Capitol police, one of his fellow patrolmen saw a woman standing at the curtains of an upstairs bedroom in an area where no unauthorized guests were allowed. When he walked over to tell her she shouldn't be in that area, she disappeared before his eyes, leaving only a scary fluttering of the curtains.

While these are the only recorded sightings of the wispy visitor, she has more frequently been heard, and, at least once, felt. "I've heard footsteps more than once and there wasn't anyone in the house but me," says one mansion security officer. A number of servants have sworn they also have heard her walking about in a "rustling taffeta gown." Once, a butler chased her down a flight of stairs into the basement, where she allegedly "escaped."

She has frequently been heard by security men as they sat at a table in the kitchen hallway in the basement. Says one officer, "Many a night I've been sitting there when the Governor and his wife are away, and I've heard doors slam and someone walking upstairs. I've gone upstairs to look, and all the doors were locked tight and no one was around."

A curious incident occurred during the tenure of Linwood Holton in 1972 that added to the ghost's credibility. When Hurricane Agnes whipped through Richmond that year, it caused a blackout downtown, including the Capitol and the Governor's Mansion. All was dark, that is except for a single lightbulb in the ladies' stairwell of the mansion. It continued shining like a beacon in the storm.

One who remembers this well is Ann Compton, ABC-TV's White House correspondent who then was on assignment at the state Capitol. She was called to the house to witness the phenomenon by one of Holton's staff secretaries. Recalls Ms. Compton: "Every light switch we tried didn't affect it. Jinx Holton (the governor's wife) always told me she thought there was a ghost. Rationally, I suppose I'd like to think it was a fluke in the wiring. Irrationally, I'd like to think I'm as romantic as most Virginians about their history and that she (the ghost) was the spirit that brought the light to the Governor's Mansion when the rest of the city was dark and wet."

As an eerie sidelight to this episode, Governor Holton later told the Richmond *Times-Dispatch* that during the blackout someone or something moved several of the paintings in his bedroom.

Whoever, or whatever, the presence is which inhabits the Governor's mansion, it apparently was real enough to scare one Capitol policeman clean out of his job. Officer Toms says this particular officer, who prefers to remain nameless, was in the basement one night when he distinctly felt something touch his face. He was so terrified, he ran out of the house, throwing down his badge along the way and quit the force. He came back only to collect his paycheck.

Once, during Governor Dalton's time in office, yet another officer had a hair-raising experience in the basement. He became curious when the Governor's dog, the hair on its back raised, barked furiously at a window. As he stepped over to investigate, he felt a frigid chill in the room. He noticed that although it was in the middle of a summer heat wave, the window had frosted over. And the curtains were swirling about madly. In a few seconds the curtains stilled and the frosting on the window disappeared.

During the time of Governor Andrew Montague, just after the turn of the 20th century, Robert Lynch and Dr. Horace Hoskins were living in the mansion. One night they both were awakened by the unmistakable sound of footsteps in their room, accompanied by the "swish of a silk skirt." They got up and followed the sound along the corridor and down the hallway below the stairs where they lost it. And according to the official "Mansion Tour Script," the brother of Governor Montague once chased the ghostly lady down a staircase and into the street.

Who is she, and why has she chosen the Governor's Mansion, of all places, to make her periodic presence known? No one has ever come up with even a hint of an answer. But it is possible that whatever her cause or curse was, it may have been appeased. For Governor Charles Robb says, "During my tenure, neither my family nor the staff have experienced any unusual sounds or sights."

Perhaps she is a Democrat, satisfied at last!

C H A P T E R 1 6

A TRAGEDY OF GOLD AND GREED

"What make him dream 'bout de goole so much, if 'taint cause he bit by de goole bug?"
— *The Gold Bug*

There is a splendid folklorian tale of greed, gold, mystery, brutal murder, and incessant hauntings worthy of Edgar Allan Poe himself, that has been passed down through generations of Goochland County natives for more than a century and a half. Like many such legends, the details have worn so thin with the passage of time that the actual names of the principals are as lost today as are the ill-gotten gains upon which the story revolves. The last accounting of this particular drama surfaced in the form of a letter to the editor of a Richmond newspaper more than 50 years ago. However, it is such an interesting — and plausible — narrative that it is worthy of retelling even if there is no way to authenticate the facts.

One gathers from the letter that the "old Waller gold mine" in Goochland County, "about 40 miles up the James River from Richmond," was reopened sometime in the early 1930s, after having been shut down and forgotten for three quarters of a century. This mine had been one of a number actively mined in the 1830s and 1840s. And, apparently, quite a horde of gold was harvested here, for the letter's author refers to Waller as being: "known the world over as the richest gold mine in America and in which was found some fabulously rich ore." So, obviously, this had to be some years before Mr. Sutter discovered the first huge nuggets in California which led to the great gold rush of 1849.

Near the Waller mine there was a large wooden frame house which has been described as being two stories high with "gray, weather-beaten boards and gaping doors and windows (which) conspire to make it far from inviting." It was still standing in the 1930s, at least, and was said then to be haunted. Further description includes a yard "within the crumbled fence, grown with tangled shrubs and weeds (which) shows that for a long time there has been an absence of human life there. Even the big chimney...assumes a lowering and suggestive look."

According to the legend, strange noises have been heard there, especially late at night. Among these are, "the despairing cry as of someone about to pass into the unknown." So scary and realistic were these sounds that the house became known as "a place where no one cares to go and where many hurry by."

It was here where several employees of Waller mine lived during its heyday. Some of them were a little bit less than honest, and secretly pocketed some of the gold. One man in particular had squirreled away a sizeable cache which he kept hidden in a secret spot near the house. One of his fellow roomers followed him one day and learned the location of the steadily building treasure trove.

A few nights later the occupants of the house were awakened by a piercing scream from the room of the man who had stolen the gold. They rushed in and found him lying unconscious on the floor. His head had been bashed in by some kind of blunt instrument. He died without gaining consciousness. A following investigation failed to turn up the slightest clue as to who killed him or why, and the case remained unsolved for many years. Waller mine subsequently ran out of the mother lode and was boarded up with the employees scattering in all directions of the map.

The roomer who had followed the employee to his hiding place met with an accident of his own years later, and, on his death bed, attempted to atone for his sin by confessing that it was, indeed, he who had murdered the man. He told how he had crept into the room that night with the intention of killing him, and that when he stepped on a creaky board in the floor, the man had risen from his bed asking, "Who's there?" He had then crashed a lethal blow upon the man's head with a pole ax. When the man screamed as he fell, his assailant ran back to his room, hid the ax, then came out and joined the others seeking the source of the scream. He later buried the . ax, and, in time, when things settled down, he dug up the hidden gold and left for the North.

But, he added, he had never enjoyed his sudden wealth. Rather, he gave a vivid account of how the dead man had relentlessly haunted him by day and by night; how he had suffered more than "a thousand deaths," and had never known a peaceful moment from the time he struck the fatal blow.

Even his last minute confession, however, did not seem to appease the spirit of his victim, for the strange noises in the old house, long vacant, continued to occur for decades afterward. Goochland County oldtimers say it was the restless ghost of the dead gold miner still searching vainly for his lost treasure.

The
Winged
Harbinger
of Doom

"The trees were dark in color, and mournful in form and attitude, wreathing themselves into sad, solemn, and spectral shapes that conveyed ideas of mortal sorrow and untimely death."
— *The Island of the Fay*

On the morning of April 3, 1865, shortly before the final meeting at Appomattox, General Robert E. Lee, along with General Longstreet and their staffs, were at Summit, a small village about 20 miles from Richmond and adjacent to Clover Hill in Chesterfield County — the ancestral home of the Cox family. Hearing of Lee's proximity, Judge James H. Cox dispatched a messenger to invite the Confederate leaders to a noon day meal.

Upon Lee's arrival, Judge Cox's daughter, saying "the uppermost thing in her mind," told the general, "We shall gain the cause. You will join General Johnson and together you will be victorious." Whereupon Lee smiled and commented, "Whatever happens, know this, that no men ever fought better than those who have stood by me."

Kate Virginia Cox remembered, too, that Lee drank ice water while the others indulged in mint juleps, and that after an "abundant dinner (for the best of everything that was left was brought out in honor of the general"), Lee put cream in his coffee. When Kate asked him about this he smiled again and replied, "I have not taken coffee for so long that I would not dare to take it in its original strength." Kate mentioned this later to one of Lee's staff, and he told her, "You know the general sends all his coffee to the hospital." Soonafter, the general mounted Traveler and was on his way, having eaten his last meal under anyone's roof until after the surrender.

Such marvelous anecdotes seem to abound at Clover Hill, which has been described in a Virginia Historic Landmarks Commission report as "one of the most historically significant plantations in Chesterfield County." Some of the legends, passed down through the years by slaves and others who have lived there, involve bizarre tragedies, and with them are associated some classic ghost stories. These include tales of a bird swooping through a window at the approach of death; an eerie rapping on a certain side door when an adult member of the family is about to die; phantoms and banshees flitting through the skeletal branches of the once-stately Lombardy poplars; mysterious deaths, including a disembodiment at an old spring; and the often-repeated story of "Cox's snow."

But first it is appropriate to set the scene with some background on the house and property. The Landmarks Commission report states simply that "this house has a complex history." Further, it says, "While the dwelling is said to have been built in 1787, there is no architectural evidence for so early a date. Two distinct segments of the house date from the early 19th century, the large two-story section was built shortly after the Civil War, and since then various one-story additions have been put on."

In contrast, Cox family records indicate, "the older wing of the house dates to the 18th century." Regardless, it is believed that James H. Cox moved to the farm known as "Winterpock," (from an old Indian name for a neighboring creek), in 1835, and sometime after that his wife changed the name to Clover Hill. Cox was the eldest son of Major Henry Cox, Sr., who served in the War of 1812. When he died in 1828, his Chesterfield County estate totalled 1,258 acres, including the land upon which the house stands. His father, in turn, was a soldier of the Revolution, Captain at Guilford Courthouse, and a signer of the Revolutionary Petition of Chesterfield County. And his father was another Henry Cox, and the first at Winterpock. He was born at Coxendale (Cox and Dale) on the James River between 1700 and 1705.

The James Henry Cox who came to Clover Hill in 1835 had graduated from Hampden-Sydney College six years earlier; had "read law" in the office of his cousin, John Winston Jones, Speaker of the U.S. House of Representatives; and, in 1832, had gone to the Territory of Florida as headmaster of Tallahassee Academy, then the largest school in Florida.

All of this is recorded in a Cox family history which is prefaced with this colorful note: "Grandmother's knee is a wonderful place to learn about the Bible, ghosts, and even Santa Claus, but a mighty poor place to learn history." Nevertheless, it is established that a rich vein of coal was discovered on the property by a slave in 1837. The productive Clover Hill Coal Mines were worked extensively during the 1800s, as were the Bright Hope and Coalboro coal pits, which became the Bright Hope Coal Company. The coal was carried to the James River on the Clover Hill Railroad.

The Clover Hill Academy for boys also was operated here during the 19th century. There were two dormitories for boys in the yard, tall, slender buildings each with one room up and one down. One stood by the goose house and the other was on the terrace. Mrs. Lewis Lush, whose husband bought the land in 1955, says there was always a school here, after the Civil War, too.

Of all the stories swirling about Clover Hill certainly the most famous concerns the great blizzard of 1857, which has become known in Chesterfield County lore as "Cox's Snow." The date was January 17, and Dr. Joseph Edwin Cox, a cousin of Henry, was called from his home in Petersburg to visit a patient in Chesterfield. According to one account of the incident, published in 1937, "It was snowing furiously, and his horse sloshed through the muck hour after hour. Finally, completely exhausted and chilled to the bone, the doctor and horse reached the gate of Clover Hill in the night. The snow was piled high about the fence posts and the wind whipped around in icy flurries . . . Ask any oldster in the county, and he will tell you that such a storm has not been seen since.

"Dr. Cox edged his numb body out of the buggy and plodded through the drifts to unlatch the gate. It was icy, frozen, immovable. He called through the black murk of falling snow. He called again and again, until his voice was a faint whisper."

Here, the story is picked up by Mrs. Jennie Patterson, a former slave at Clover Hill born about 1846, who was interviewed when she was 91 years old. She was about 11 years old at the time. "I was up yonder in de big house, settin' knittin' socks fer my marster. Dr. Cox . . . had been drinkin' heavy dat day when he came from Petersburg. When he got most to de house, we heard him callin' but thought t'was some of de t'other folks 'round dar. His daughter (Mrs. Grimes), wouldn't git up to open de do' 'cause we all was gittin' ready to go to bed."

The next morning slaves found Dr. Cox near the gate frozen to death. As Jennie Patterson recalled it: "I seed him dar when dey all went out. Fus' seed his horse an' buggy comin' to de house dout (without) nobody in hit. All got scared an' went a-searchin' an' callin' him. An' lo' an' behold, dar was Marse Cox stiff in de snow. Chile, I'se been feard to tell all I know 'bout dis here thing. Dar's bin all kinds of tales de white folks bin all kiverin' hit over. Marse Cox liked his liquors so he was drunk an' couldn' make hit, not bein' of his self. I bet you ain' heard dat. Yes, yes, dar was a big bother-ation at de big house. Naw, I ain' said nothin' 'tall 'bout dem ghost.''

What the ex-slave wouldn't refer to, was what has hap-pened at Clover Hill ever since. "Sperrits," some of the former servants called them. The phenomenon involves a specific upstairs bedroom. Something, or someone — the most commonly offered explanation is that it is the ghost of frozen Dr. Cox — "keeps watch over the bedroom in a most discomfiting (sic) manner." He will not let the sleeper keep any bedcover on himself after midnight, especially if he is the only person in the place.

There apparently is some credibility to this because it is told that once a certain "minister of the gospel (whose word, naturally, goes unquestioned)" spent the night there and was "so harried by this persistent ghost that he grabbed a blanket and spent the night out of doors."

There are a host of other hauntings at Clover Hill, some fanciful, some more difficult to explain away by rational means. For example, cedars now line the old carriage drive, where once tall Lombardy poplars stood. In pre-Civil War days slaves believed "Haidless ho'semen" rode at night among them. Looking at the shimmering branches on dark nights, the slaves said they saw "folks made out o' bones wid wings, an' hants flappin' roun'!" They made such a hue and cry that Judge Cox had the trees cut down.

Then there are the gruesome stories of the spring from which fresh water was drawn for the house. Ex-slave Jennie Patterson: "Dar was a slave amongst us who 'cided to run away an' a 'oman slave heard him doin' his plan. She ups an' tells her mistress, an' mistress sends dis man to de spring to fetch water. Down dat spring dar was dem overseers. De man stayed so long fo' he brought de water up to de house (that) another slave went to look for him an' do you know dat man was found all cut up in de water bucket. Yes, dem buckets was big buckets; no setch buckets like you see now."

In all probability, Jennie's tale has been considerably embellished in the retelling, and the land owners probably did nothing to discourage it because fear was one of the best resources in keeping slaves from running away. Still, there was something mysterious abut the spring because there is a much better documented account of what happened there to another slave, Aunt Jensie. She was dispatched one day to the spring for water and when she failed to come back they found her head and upper torso in the water, "dead as a doornail." So profound was the terror among the servants after that, that none would go to the spring again for water, even under the threat of a whipping. Subsequently, the spring was bricked up and never used again.

Several members of the Cox family have died suddenly at Clover Hill, and each time, servants say, it was preceded by a harbinger of death. This took the form of a "sharp rapping" on a particular side door of the house. While there is little to substantiate this legend, there is a fairly detailed remembrance of the "swooping bird" who made a sign of death.

It was during the early days of the War between the States. One evening in early October, Judge James H. Cox was "taking his ease in the double parlors." His three sons had recently left to join the Confederate Army, and he was alone in the room. He heard "a fluttering of wings, 'tis said, and instantly a small dark bird circled about his head, then flew out the window."

In a few days the judge and his wife and daughter left for Norfolk, where Edwin, the favorite son, was stationed. The servants said they made the trip, " 'cause de bird had done gib de sign." They found the boy "thin and rosy-cheeked with the flush of ill health." The family brought him back to Clover Hill, where his health became worse. He died the day after Christmas, and was laid out in the parlor where the bird had appeared.

The Coxes called the death, after the appearance of the bird, a coincidence. The servants had another name for it. It was "hants," they said.

THE BAFFLING CASE OF THE BROODING NUN

"The boundaries which divide Life from Death are at best shadowy and vague."

— *The Premature Burial*

In Salem, Massachusetts, centuries ago, fear so overcame town residents that they publicly burned witches. And in Richmond, approximately 100 years ago, there is a recorded instance where citizens were so terrorized at the specter of "a woman in a window" that they eventually demolished a house on Fifth Street in an effort to rid themselves of the haunting apparition.

This was, in the annals of psychic phenomena, a highly unusual case, because the ghost was "seen" not by a single person, or a handful of people. It was witnessed by thousands! In fact, when word spread about town of the mysterious woman, the abandoned house became somewhat of a tourist attraction, much to the consternation of a local real estate agent who was trying to sell it.

Although the legend was passed rapidly through the community by word of mouth, probably with a new layer of embellishment in each recounting, the facts of the occurrence were set in print in June 1890 by a newspaper columnist identified only as "Felix." Here, in part, is what he wrote:

"Late upon a shadowy evening. . . a young man was walking out Fifth Street, when some uncertain distance beyond Leigh (Street), where the houses are all grey and tottering with unkept old age, he absently turned his gaze upon a vacant and silent looking house. At an upper window his astonished eyes discerned the solemn face of a sad-eyed, hooded nun peering out. He stopped and looked long and carefully, but no closer scrutiny proved an error in his sight or impression. Unmoved, and with melancholy steadiness, the solemn eyes of the nun looked down at him from out their frame of black veiling, looked beseechingly and longingly until he was conscious of no impulse but to release a prisoner, who seemed to be one by some strange chance or accident, so he bounded up the dust-ladened, trackless steps to try the front door in vain.

"A yellow, rain-smeared card, tacked upon the wall, told that it (the house) was 'For Sale.' The ragged, overgrown weeds choked the side entrance to the yard, but forcing that, he bravely tried to get in the back way, but the locks, at least, were still on duty and resisted his efforts. It was growing late then, so he again walked around and looked up at the window, to see in the gathering darkness the same face of the beseeching, saint-like nun at the window.

"Still believing it to be a human being imprisoned, he sought the agent of the deserted house and told his story, but he only found an incredulous listener, who assured him that it was nonsense, that that was 'one of the most desirable houses in town, nice and quiet, away from the bustle and noise, yet convenient to business.' Having thundered out this formula of his business, which is kept in readiness like a ready-loaded cartridge to fire off at whatever rises in the field, he thought the matter ended. But the young man was importunate, and finally persuaded him to get the keys of the house and to go with him, and if he confessed to seeing the face there they both would go in and make a search.

"Even by the stingy, pale light of the moon and a fitful lantern they carried, the agent, too, could not help seeing that in verity there was the face of a nun pressed close to the glass and looking out. They entered bravely, with the heavy, forward tread which marched over the carpetless floor and rickety stairs and resounded in all the empty space with some sound akin to echo, but the heart of each fluttered with an unmanly nervousness that neither of them would have liked to confess.

"They, however, came to the room from whose window the face peered, confidently expecting to there find a miserable, frightened woman for them to release and remove to some more cheerful quarters. They entered, and the ray of the lantern fell directly upon the window they came to search, but it only fell upon a vacant, cobwebbed sill, and lit with a sickly, pallid shine the empty, glaring window panes. No so much as a shadow did the lantern there reveal, but only the weird shine of the dim, smoky light on the glass.

"There seemed an insufferable silence in the room, and

something more dread than fright seemed to make it impossible for either of them to speak a word. They moved about the room, but even their foot treads had a smothered, distant, far-away sound, and while neither of them could discern the faintest trace of any object in the room, however, after they turned the lantern in the corners and around its walls, there was a strong feeling with each that there was something undefined, which moved around with them just sufficiently to disturb the waves of air that came in contact with their bodies.

"They left the house without further search that night, both of them more unstrung and over wrought than they knew. The next day in the full glare of the noon-tide sun, in the unimaginative clearness of afternoon light, or at whatever hour of the day that one looked, there was to be seen that same unmovable steady, pleading stare of the solemn black veiled nun.

"It did not take many hours for the news of the advent of the strange and sudden apparition to spread. The neighborhood was in a riotous state of nervous tumult, and fled the vicinity with more rapidity than if the small-pox flag had hung from the window instead of the shadow image of a pale-faced, sad-eyed woman.

"From morning until night crowds of curious and awe-stricken people gathered around the house, thousands sometimes going a day to look at the haunted window. Some few were brave enough to explore the room, the incredulous ones, but such would come out trembling and convinced. There were a few attempts made to burn the disturbing phantom home, after which policemen were placed on continuous guard. The reporters had a 'Widow's Crew's' supply of material, and interesting matter seemed to increase for them regarding it day by day.

"At last it was thought expedient to tear down and ruthlessly destroy such a useless element of annoyance and mental discord. From the heavy felling blows of the pick-axe and the spade, the haunted house was mutilated and the sad-eyed, solemnly-veiled nun shattered in her image existence upon the window pane and (was) driven back into her proper sphere, in the shades of some deserted cloister, or the clammy realms of a ceiled vault, where she could look out through rusted iron bars and win the sympathy of bats and owls, while peace once again reigned on Fifth Street, and despair ceased its hold upon the mind of the real estate agent."

C H A P T E R   1 9

SPECTRAL
SIGHTINGS

"When I first beheld this apparition — for I could scarcely regard it as less — my wonder and my terror were extreme."
— The Black Cat

Some ghosts are persistant. They haunt a particular house for years, decades, generations, even centuries in some instances. Some stay with certain families, and when these families move or pass on, the wraiths disappear never to return. Only rarely, however, is a case recorded where the ghost is seen, felt or heard just once, and then for barely a few fleeting seconds. In Richmond, this has happened twice — one involving an apparition which appeared more than three-quarters of a century ago, and the other much more recently.

* * * * * *

In most instances, those who experience "a sighting" see more of a vague, wispy outline than anything else. This usually has a shadowy, foggish appearance. Sometimes, just the outline of the head is envisioned; more often a head and shoulders; and, once in a while, a full-length figure. Almost always "it" is white or opaque, and the odds are it generally is a woman. It is unusual for any features to be distinct. They are mostly misty or hazy and difficult to bring into sharp focus.

Such was not the situation in the singular experience of Captain Jeffry Montague, a former city editor of the *Richmond News-Leader*, who confronted a ghost one evening in the year 1908 in his brick residence on Franklin Street. His account of the encounter has been well documented, not only by himself, but by Margaret DuPont Lee in "Virginia Ghosts," and by several other writers. Nevertheless, it is worth recounting here because of the clarity of the vision, the vivid details as recalled by a trained journalist, and the fact that the spiritual manifestation happened only once, and then only to Captain Montague and to no one else in the house.

Here is how he described the incident: "My wife slept in the back room and I at the front of the house, in the top story. The door in the partition wall between the two rooms was open; doors of both rooms into the hall were open; the windows both front and rear were open. I was awakened sometime between 2:30 and 3 o'clock in the morning by a roaring sound, which, as I became conscious, resolved itself into the noise of an automobile going east on Franklin Street at high speed. I had not moved as I listened to this noise.

"Suddenly I felt sharply aware that someone else was in the room. The natural thought 'burglar' sprang into my mind. I opened my eyes just enough for vision. Standing about a yard from the foot of my bed was the figure of a woman. The head and shoulders were distinctly outlined, but the rest of the figure was a white blur. I really do not know how to describe accurately the surface appearance of this figure.

"It seemed like a million tiny, dull, unpolished pearls laid together. I thought, of course, it was my wife, awakened by the noise and come into my room to look out of the window. In her childhood she had sometimes walked in her sleep. I had always heard it was dangerous to awaken a sleep walker suddenly; therefore, I kept perfectly still and watched the figure through eyelids almost closed. The figure stood another five or ten seconds apparently looking at me and then turned and moved towards one of the two front windows, the one farthest from my bed.

"I thought nothing of it at the time, but recalled later that it did not walk as a living person would. It seemed to float to the window. This later impressed me as strange, however, because my wife was of a substantial mould and walked with a distinct characteristic motion. The figure, upon reaching the window, inclined its head and looked down into the street.

Now, for the first time, features were recognizable. They were the nose and chin. The nose, well shaped and of good size, clearly topped the lower indoor blinds, which were closed and latched. The upper indoor blinds were open and so was the upper sash. There were no outside blinds."

Captain Montague continued his narrative: "I had risen cautiously upon my elbow while this was going on. I watched the figure while it gazed into the street, wondering what I should do, if anything. The figure now turned and came back to the foot of my bed, where it stood facing me. Still thinking it was my wife, I was convinced now that she was sleep walking, because if she were awake, she would speak, seeing me raised up on my elbow looking at her.

"Very gently, so as not to alarm her, I murmured her name, 'Hally.' Instantly, the figure sank to the floor, disappearing in the blackness at the foot of my bed. The fall or disappearance was noiseless, but I did not notice that at the moment. Shocked and anxious, fearing a serious consequence to my wife, I sprang up, hurried to the mantel over the fireplace opposite my bed, groped for a match and lighted the gas. There was no one on the floor! I looked hastily around the room. No one was there.

"In another moment I was in my wife's room, and there she was in her bed, apparently just awakened by the flash of light and the commotion I was making in my search.

" 'Hally! You here?' I exclaimed incredulously; a silly enough question, of course, for there she was. 'Where else should I be at this time of night?' she responded.

" 'Weren't you in my room just now looking out of the window?'

" 'I certainly was not. Your light waked me up. What is the matter with you?'

"For the first time it dawned upon me that I had seen a ghost. I told her what had happened and asked her if she would get up, come into my room and do exactly what I told her to do. She agreed, with the idea of humoring a harmless lunatic. She was in a long plain white nightgown. I placed her standing where I had first seen the ghost, turned out the light and got back into bed. She was invisible! The white of her nightgown did not show at all. I could hardly discern the dark outline of her figure. The ghostly substance, therefore, while not radiant, had been luminous!

"I asked her to go to the far window and look out. She turned towards the window and was stopped by a large Morris chair, and asked me facetiously what she should do — climb over the chair or walk around it. I told her to go around it. Arrived at the window, she was unable to look out over the lower blind, the top of which was above her head!

"I remained awake for some time, hoping that the spirit would reappear, but it did not. I never saw it again. I believe firmly that that night I saw the ghost which haunts that old brick house on Franklin Street, Richmond, Virginia."

* * * * * *

Mildred Whitfield of Chesterfield County had an experience similar to Captain Montague's, only hers occurred much more recently, in 1981, and possibly again in the summer of 1984. Possibly, because Mildred is not certain if her second encounter was actually a sighting or the result of a dream. In either case there are some distinctions between what she saw or perceived to see and what Montague witnessed. First, her ghost definitely was a male, maybe two males. Secondly, while Montague could offer no reason for the appearance of his wraith-like figure, Mildred says there are a couple of conceivable explanations for hers.

She was standing in the kitchen of her historic home, called Railey Hill and located just off Route 60 in Midlothian, one evening a few minutes before midnight, when she glanced around and saw "it." In her words: "It came floating across the breakfast room. It was like a form. I saw what I thought was the shape of a man's face. I screamed to my husband, Carl, to come quick. Then I ran after it. I wasn't afraid of it in the least. But when I got to the corner it was gone. It had simply disappeared. It may have gone down into the cellar, but I don't know. The door was shut. Carl didn't see it. He just shakes his head and laughs at me when I talk about it, but I swear I saw it, and it was a ghost.

"Then in the summer of 1984, I was in bed one night when

I saw another white form at the foot of my bed. Only this time it appeared to be the form of a young boy, a sort of small chunky white form. I rose up from the bed and it vanished down into the floor. There was nothing there. I may have been dreaming, but I don't think so. It was too real."

The Whitfields have lived at Railey Hill for more than 30 years, and have painstakingly restored the house. "When we bought it, it was in pretty bad shape," Mildred says. "There was tar paper on the floors. We had it removed and had the floors refinished. It had stood empty for many years and some people in the area had referred to it as the haunted house.

"Railey Hill has nine rooms and eight fireplaces," she adds, and the original floors are of Virginia heart pine. Inside are "witch doors," each with a large cross in them. Mildred says in the early days of the 19th century it was believed that such doors kept witches from crossing the threshold.

In her research into the history of the house, she learned that it had been built about 1800, perhaps earlier, by a Mr. Railey who came from England to open the Railey Coal Mines in Midlothian. He designed the house after his English home. Mildred found some clues to the possible identity of the specters she saw. The first one, she feels, could be the return of a young Yankee officer who lived in the house in 1865.

The following words are etched into a window pane in the parlor: "Lt. Charles F. Branch, U.S. Army, address Orwell, Vermont 1865." He is said to have led the first group of Union soldiers to the area during the fall of Richmond. His troop of 100 was sent ahead of the siege to occupy and protect the valuable coal mines in the area. Mildred was told the lieutenant loved the house and used a diamond to carve his message on the parlor window pane.

As to the younger spirit, Mildred says a superintendent of the coal mines was living in the house in the early 1800s, and he lost his 12-year-old son in a mining accident. "Others have seen a boy ghost in the Walton Park area, so that's why I think it may have been him," she says.

"Actually, the funny thing is I don't believe in ghosts, but I know I saw something."

THE MULTIPLE HAUNTS OF REVEILLE

"And travellers now, within that valley,
Through the red-litten windows see
Vast forms, that move fantastically
To a discordant melody..."
— The Haunted Palace

There is some apparent confusion over the origins of Reveille, a magnificent old Federal-style country house located on Cary Street Road in the west end of Richmond behind the Reveille United Methodist Church. According to one report filed by the Virginia Historic Landmarks Commission, it is, "a handsome example of an early 19th-century" house. However, the same document qualifies this by adding, "the actual date of erection and the builder of Reveille are uncertain. It is known from the 19th century diary of Miss Rebecca Williams that her family lived in the house circa 1806, when it was rented...the prototype for Reveille is found in houses that were erected in the city of Richmond circa 1790 to 1820. It is unfortunate that most of the salient examples have been destroyed."

Others believe the house is much older. In one article in the *Richmond Times Dispatch* written more than 60 years ago, it is stated that Reveille, then known as the "Brick House," had "already become a landmark." Still another article refers to

Reveille as "one of the oldest houses in Richmond" and, "is viewed as more original in its structure than any other in the city except possibly the Poe Shrine." This article says it could have been built as early as 1720 on a land grant from the King of England to the Kennon family.

In a history of Reveille, written by Emily Tapscott Clark in 1920, she says, "Members of the Kennon family were among the great landholders of Henrico County. . . in the early part of the 18th century. Dr. Slaughter, in his 'History of Bristol Parish,' says that between 1670 and 1760, grants were made to various Kennons to the extent of 50,000 acres, and the property known as the 'Brick House Tract' (Reveille) was large . . . It appears that the history of the house during the Kennon regime is more or less misty." Ms. Clark further says, "Turner Southall was master of the house shortly after the Revolution, for his will was admitted to probate June 6, 1791."

While there may be continued debate over exactly when the house was built, there is no argument as to its enduring beauty. In the urban sprawl that has encroached upon Reveille's once-rural setting, it remains an island monument to the simple yet glorious past that was Virginia 200 years ago.

What Ms. Clark wrote so many years ago, holds true today: "But it is on entering the wide hall that the enchantment of Reveille is most keenly felt. More than one distinguished architect from New York and Boston has been moved to spontaneous enthusiasm by the simple perfection of this hall, and the rooms opening into it. The beautiful old stairway, with its delicate tracery following the steps, the broad, low doors, and, especially the rosetted moldings over the windows, all bear witness to the master craftsmen of the past. In the second room to the right of the hall the high, deep windows are especially fine, and all the rooms are exquisitely proportioned. The ivory woodwork and mantels, too, are worthy of close consideration.

"Quaintest of all are the low-pitched basement rooms, whose walls are of a European thickness. The early owners of the house might easily have fortified themselves against red men or Red Coats in this vault-like place. Its cupboards, its fireplaces and tensils are fascinating, as well as its immense wine keg, and the alluring October scent of apples pervades the entire floor."

Ms. Clark says that Edgar Allan Poe was once a guest at Reveille, and that the great naturalist Audubon was a frequent visitor when he stayed with his friend, General Richardson, across the road at Windsor. She writes further that, "the small, high-set windows of the basement look out on a dim, bricked space below the porch, and the gray dusk there makes one realize the necessity for the crosses so carefully marked upon the paneled doors." These, interestingly, "were carved there nearly 200 years ago by workmen who were loyal to the lords of the manor, to keep the witches away."

They may have done the job with witches, but not with ghosts, for Reveille has had more than its share of mysterious haunts down through the years. First, to set the scene, there is an authentic secret chamber in the house. It is so secret, in fact, that generations of owners didn't even know it existed. It was rediscovered early in the 20th century only when several boxes were removed into the garrett below it. It can be entered only through a hole in the attic ceiling. One must climb a ladder to this trapdoor, then crawl through a narrow hole cut in a hand-hewn beam running the length of the house. The chamber is about five by 10 feet long and eight feet deep. There are no doors or windows. It was built as a hiding place from Indians.

Secondly, as a further enticement for the reappearance of spirits, there have been some tragic and unusual deaths at Reveille. Elizabeth Crutchfield Blair was the last descendent and heiress of the house. She died in 1949. Sometime before that the family chauffeur shot and killed her husband as he was going to play golf.

Much earlier in the lore of Reveille is the story of the beautiful "daughter of the house, presumably a Kennon," who ran down the steep flight of stone steps one night to meet her lover. He was waiting outside with two horses to elope with her. Midway down the steps she tripped on the long skirt of her riding habit, and fell headlong to her death. Her grave can still be seen at the back of the garden, or at least it

could earlier in the century.

Hers is one of the ghosts, for it is said that on moonlit nights, the riderless horses may still be heard galloping madly around the house. It possibly is "her," too, who "glides" through the trapdoor, "steals through the attic and down the winding stairs to the second floor, where it usually pauses." According to Ms. Clark's account, "the swish of a skirt, too soft to be called a rustle, is heard outside the door of the large front room to the right of the hall, for this is pre-eminently the haunted room."

Ms. Clark adds that once a guest at Reveille, "who is a woman of well-known veracity, and who had the honor to be assigned to (the large front) room, was awakened in the still midnight by the knob of her door being turned. Someone crossed the floor and investigated the immense mahogany wardrobe, which seems to have a special lure for ghosts. But when the guest switched on her light the visitor had departed. Nor was she in the least alarmed for as she declares, it was unmistakably 'a friendly ghost.' "

Not everyone believed in the harmlessness of such goings on, however. There was one servant in particular who steadfastly refused to sleep in the house "lest he encounter a 'hant.'" Further, during a period early in the 19th century when the house was vacant, it is said people went out of their way not to walk near the house because it was "known to be haunted. White shapes were often seen flitting past the windows."

This probably occurred in the early 1830s, because after Turner Southall died in 1791, says a Virginia Historic Landmarks Commission report, there was "some confusion as to the ultimate disposition of his estate. The estate became the subject of much family dissension and litigation. Finally, on May 18, 1831, a decree of the Henrico County Court ordered that a public auction of the tract of land called 'the Brick House' be held on the premises and sold to the highest bidder...The notice stated that it contained 60 acres and suggested that the Brick House, at moderate expense, might be repaired and made a desirable place for a family residing in town to retire during the summer months." The statement implies that the house was neglected from the time of the estate litigation to 1831, when it was sold at auction.

There also is a report, in a history of Reveille House by Karen McLeod, that said, "many see a British soldier hanging from the tree." In Ms. McLeod's monograph, she declares that the girl who was killed falling down the stairs was wearing a "wedding gown," not a riding habit, which may better explain the swish of the skirt that has been heard in the halls.

And, finally, there was an account, written in the Sunday magazine section of the *Richmond Times Dispatch* nearly half a century ago, which declared that "a veritable colony of ghosts reside at that loveliest of Tuckahoe homes, Reveille." The author wrote that, "one of the bedrooms appears to be the meeting place of a company of ghosts, heard, but never seen. They arouse a feeling of intense interest, but inspire no terror, for they seem oblivious to everything except their own affairs.

"Imprisoned in an old wardrobe is a ghost who beats a frantic tattoo on the doors, while, on the stairs, leading to the attic, the rustle of starched skirts is heard against the rails. To complete the ghostly inhabitants of this charming home, there is the old lady, dressed in a long cape and bonnet, who never emerges from the basement dining room. She busies herself with papers in a closet, paying no heed to anyone in the room, being apparently completely self-centered with an undisclosed mission in mind and with all too little time in which to perform it."

When Elizabeth Crutchfield Blair died in 1949, she bequeathed the house to the Association for the Preservation of Virginia Antiquities. Her will stated, "As destruction follows in the wake of progress, most of the early houses of Richmond are gone. Therefore, I wish to preserve, if possible, one small bit of architecture and planting which characterizes the early years of Whiteman's life in Virginia." The Association, however, voted not to accept the house, feeling it would be too expensive to maintain, especially since Mrs. Blair stipulated that the house and grounds were "not to be changed."

The house was bought by the Reveille United Methodist Church in 1951. It is used today as administrative offices for the church. There is a print shop, storage area and a conference room on the ground floor. The first, or main floor has been maintained in period, including the parlor, dining room and a kitchen. The second and third floors now contain office complexes.

Dr. Hasbrouck Hughes, pastor of the church, says he and his staff are aware of the ghostly legends. "We do a lot of joking about it," he says, "but as far as I know, no one here has ever experienced any psychic phenomena since we have been in the house. We haven't heard any footsteps or skirts swishing, or seen any apparitions."

It is as if the ghosts of Reveille, satisfied with the church occupancy of the house, have retired.

THE APPARITION AT ANDERSON HOUSE

"He had vanished, no one could tell how, and not even the ghost of him has ever been seen since."

—X-ing a Paragrab

The old Anderson House at 103 West Franklin Street is no longer standing. Despite some valiant attempts by those interested in historic preservation, it was razed in 1970 and the site was made into a parking lot next to the Jefferson Hotel.

At the time it was demolished, Tucker Hill, architectural historian for the Virginia Historic Landmarks Commission, speaking with a sense of frustration, said: "Everyone is so proud of the historic quality of Richmond, but no one is willing to make an effort to preserve even a hint of it. 'You can't save them all,' seems to be the philosophy of Richmonders who allow historic areas to be torn down one by one."

Hill said the house would be missed not only for its beauty, but also for the gap it would leave in the facade of Franklin Street. He said its size bridged the height gap between the Jefferson and lower buildings along the street. Another thing that has been missed since its demise is the ghost of Anderson House.

The structure was built in 1816 by Carter Page and was

purchased in 1880 by Col. Archer Anderson, who had the home extensively rebuilt and enlarged in the Victorian style. He retained one of the most attractive original features of the house, however — a semi-circular, two-story portico facing the garden.

Anderson was president of the Tredegar Iron Works, and his father owned a house next door where the Jefferson Hotel now stands. In fact, the two branches of the Anderson family occupied the entire block from Franklin Street to Main Street with the two homes, gardens and stables. The colonel's house remained in the family until the late 1960s, when Mrs. Kathleen Anderson Bourland, his youngest daughter, died.

For a time it was converted into a dormitory for Virginia Commonwealth University students, and it was during this period that the alleged ghost of Col. Anderson appeared. Coeds claimed he stalked about the house late at night, making his presence known by creating a sudden chill and by smoking a phantom cigar. Several VCU students swore they smelled the distinct odor of cigar smoke on a number of occasions.

"It happened to me," said Jane Duck, a student from Lynchburg. "I was very much absorbed in the book I was reading, which had nothing to do with ghosts, when I suddenly felt chilled. Then I smelled the smoke. It was weird."

There were other haunting manifestations, too. Music and laughter was heard coming from the third floor when no one was up there. A few coeds reported feeling the touch, or brush of a hand. And then there were the digging noises. They came from beside the house. Legend has it that an underground tunnel once connected Anderson House with another structure across the street, also owned at one time by the colonel. Although the tunnel was never found, two girls did discover what may have been the tunnel's entrance. They found a circular hole, covered by a fitted wooden cover, in the basement of the house. Was someone buried alive there years ago, and are the sounds those of some weary being trying to dig itself free?

Whatever it was that frightened the VCU students, the spirit of Col. Anderson himself, or someone else, it apparently was quieted forever when the old house was torn down. There have been no reports of any strange noises, odors or chills in the area since.

LEGENDS LOST IN TIME

"And then — then all is mystery and terror, and a tale which should not be told."

—*Berenice*

Some ghost stories are difficult to track down. People who have personally witnessed psychic phenomena die or move away. Houses get torn down and paved over. Legends fade from memory. In our scientific century of moon rockets and computers on every desk, tales of hauntings and supernatural happenings seem out of place and some people feel embarrassed to relate them today for fear of being thought foolish.

For these and other reasons, a number of Richmond's more colorful specters cannot be pinned down or documented to a satisfactory degree. One hears of leads to interesting tales; snippets of manifestations. But details are lacking. Still, herewith are a few of these fragmentary stories. They are presented in rough, incomplete form because despite their brevity they are entertaining. Perhaps a reader will know more clues that may some day unlock the secrets to these antique mysteries. Read on.

* * * * *

Possibly the most famous house involved in this category is Dooley Mansion, located in Maymont Park. This was once the estate of a wealthy entrepreneur, Major James Henry Dooley and his wife, Sallie May Dooley, from whose maiden name the park's name was derived. From wealth he gained largely through railroad investments, Dooley purchased a 94-acre dairy farm on the rolling hills above the fall line of the

James River, and there he built his castle. The grounds, the estate buildings, and the interior of the mansion all embody the eclectic taste of the 19th century, a romantic period that revived and adapted historical and picturesque styles. The house was designed by Edgerton S. Rogers in the neo-Romanesque style, with a massive sandstone facade accented by pink granite columns. Turrets and towers lend a medieval aura to the structure.

After the Dooleys died, the estate was bequeathed, in 1925, to the City of Richmond to become a museum and park. A dozen or so years ago, while a restoration of the house was underway, several people working there reported strange happenings. They felt a "presence."

One, Ragan Reaves, said, "there was always the notion . . . that we were rarely actually alone. . . that there was something which tolerated us. Many times I thought I saw something — for example, a woman in a light dress or wrapper with dark blonde hair at one of the third floor windows as I checked the house before leaving for the day." But she found no one there.

Another member of the restoration staff, Bonnie Biggs, said she felt as if she had startled someone upon entering the locked and closed house on more than one morning. She described glimpsing "the tip of a woman's skirt," which vanished around a corner. Ms. Biggs also said objects in Mrs. Dooley's bedroom — the Swan Room, named after the motif of the furniture — were moved. "We got into arguments over that, with everyone denying having rearranged anything."

Ellen Rainey of the Richmond Recreation and Parks Department, which supervised the restoration, agreed that those working at the house at the time "felt something there."

Those at Dooley Mansion today, however, say they have not experienced any such phenomena.

* * * * *

Twin Oaks is a metal-roofed frame house on Monument Avenue that reportedly was built about 1800, with additions being made by the Skipwith family in the 1920s. A number of curious occurrences have taken place here. One former owner, the late Donald B. Wiltshire, Sr., said he once saw "a little man with a chin beard" on the staircase. Wiltshire was so startled, he fell. He commissioned a historian to research and write a history of the house, but never did learn the identity of his mysterious visitor.

He did discover, though, that Twin Oaks was used as a hospital during the Civil War, and is supposed to have 19 bodies buried somewhere on the grounds. One legend that has persisted concerns a treasure of $500,000 hidden somewhere on the original 240 acres. The money was allegedly buried by a bank employee who had been accused in a mid-19th century theft. Wiltshire once began a search for the money under the house, but gave up when he discovered an 18-inch concrete foundation.

A later owner, Mrs. L. Vaden Scott said that she and her husband have been unable to explain several instances of objects moving from place to place. They have, for example, found small Japanese figurines moved from shelf to shelf in glass-enclosed cases. Also, Mrs. Scott apparently had lost a prized sweater when she moved into the house. She had searched everywhere for it in vain. Then one evening she found a sleeve of the sweater protruding in a closet, as if to say, 'here I am.'

* * * * *

The ubiquitous Dr. Donald Rhinesmith, who experienced psychic phenomena while living in Glasgow House, also found a spirit of sorts at his home, Avondale. The older section of this house, about 10 miles north of Richmond, was built in 1820, with a wing added in 1835.

In June 1966, shortly after buying the house, Rhinesmith was working there one night on electrical plans when he heard a loud rapping at a large double door which was once the main entrance to the house, but is no longer used. He opened the door, but no one was there. At 4 a.m. the knock came again, and there still was no one there.

The following year, within a day of the date he first heard it, Rhinesmith again heard the rapping. "I dashed to the door, threw it open, but there wasn't a sign that anything or anyone had even been there," he recalls. He never heard the knocking at any other time except between June 3 and 5, but he can't explain why. "It isn't a tapping. It's a distinct, insistent knocking."

Both he and his wife have heard faint music late at night coming from the oldest part of the house. "The music is very muted, but it seems to be a classical form — a pianoforte or harpsichord, perhaps. Sometimes there is an overlay of what seem to be voices," he says.

* * * * *

Another site whose name has faded from memory, and was described only as "a lovely old home on the Upper James, set amid great trees of a park," housed the ghost of a young boy. This incident also was written long ago by a woman named Beryl Thomas. She wrote that the walls of the house were covered with portraits of generations of the family, "whose members have distinguished themselves in the making of Virginia history."

Among the portraits was a charming group of three children, a girl and two boys, dressed in the fashion of a by-gone day. The youngest of the group, a boy of about six, grew to manhood, but died "in his 30th year."

According to the author, this house had been long famed for its genial hospitality and happy family life. Ms. Thomas wrote: "When laughter rings through the rooms the young man (re)appears, not as he left his terrestrial home, but as a child in the precise apparel shown in the little portrait.

"He coyly peeps around doors, his bright little face reflecting the mirth in which he obviously so ardently wishes to join. When detected, he scampers down the hall and disappears from sight. He is, indeed, a merry little ghost whose life, for him, had naught but happy memories of his sheltered and loving childhood."

* * * * *

A few years ago a woman wrote an account in a national magazine of ghostly manifestations she experienced at her house which she described only as being in Mechanicsville. She said "an unknown hand" began to turn doorknobs and toss bottles. Mail left on the kitchen table disappeared, then reappeared on the table several weeks later. Once a houseguest's bracelet was missing and thorough searches turned up nothing. Then, several days later the bracelet "materialized" on a counter in plain sight.

An old bottle set on the kitchen mantel was found smashed on the floor in an opposite corner of the room, and a pitcher "voluntarily" fell off a wall hook and shattered, although the hook was still firmly in place. There also were strange odors, acrid and smoky, whose source could never be detected. Curiously, all these incidents occurred in just two rooms of the house — the kitchen and the guest bedroom above it.

Others felt a presence, too. A visiting in-law was frightened by heavy footsteps on the stairs and a loud thumping. A repairman one day found a back door flung open — one that was always locked with a dead bolt for which no one had ever found the key! He left in a haste without asking any questions.

The woman brought in a psychic who told her the ghost was that of a woman named "Dora" who died in the house about 1812. Other psychics came and one said that the specter had died violently. Then he asked if there had ever been a fire in the house. The house owner said that the wood beams in the kitchen walls and ceiling were badly charred. Then she shuddered as she remembered the time she sensed the acrid smell of burning that had wafted through the house.

* * * * *

Then there is the shadowy story of the tragic ghost of the Liggon House at 2601 E. Franklin Street. No one seems to recall the exact details, but the gist goes something like this. John L. Liggon was a prominent Richmond tobacco manufacturer. The house dates to 1857.

Allegedly, some members of the Liggon family were going into town one afternoon to do some shopping. There was a little girl, probably five or six years old at the time. She told a black male servant that they were going to town, but that he couldn't go with them. Just before they were to leave, the little girl saw the servant walking down the stairs of the house all dressed up. She got one of her father's pistols, said, "I told you you couldn't go," and shot him dead.

For years after that, his apparition could be seen descending the stairs.

* * * * *

And finally, there is the unsolved mystery of the "Chiles Place," in Chesterfield County. This was described by Margaret DuPont Lee in her classic book, "Virginia Ghosts," published in 1930. This house was said to have been built prior to 1800. Sometime around 1875, the Chiles family members began being disturbed by "strange noises." Locked doors would fly open. Shuttered windows could not be kept shut, and fastened windows would raise by themselves. And there were unexplained whisperings and soft step movements.

One evening in particular proved eerie. With several Chiles sitting in the living room before the fireplace, the sounds of someone tiptoeing down the stairs were distinctly heard. A search found no one. No sooner had everyone regathered in the living room when the sounds were heard again. A thorough investigation of the entire house proved futile. Then, the solid oak bars bolting the front and back doors crashed to the floor and the doors flew open.

Such manifestations went on for some time, but no explanation was ever found, even though one member of the family offered $1,000 to anyone who would spend a night in the house and determine the true source.

To add to this mystery, no record of a house known as the Chiles Place can be found. The house and the ghost within it apparently have vanished from Chesterfield County!

SOME FAMOUS "NON-GHOSTS"

"We are surely doomed to hover continually upon the brink of eternity, without taking a final plunge into the abyss."
— *Ms. Found in a Bottle*

One of the most curious facts about Richmond is the number of sites that are *not* haunted. In the rich lore of the city there have been many strange and often tragic occurrences of which anyone who has made even a cursory study of psychic phenomena would be inclined to associate with ghosts. In each of these cases, based on what is known about the spirit world, there is every reason for an ethereal presence, yet, inexplicably, none has surfaced.

Chronologically, for example, one could go back more than 300 years ago, when a band of Iroquois Indians, down from New York state, encamped at a site near Libby Terrace, on a bluff in Church Hill, off Franklin Street. The ravine below this point is now called "Sugar Bottom." It once was known, however, as "Bloody Run."

It was here, in 1656, that some of our Colonial forefathers, along with the Pamunkey Indians, attacked the Iroquois. The settlers and Pamunkeys, including their chief, Totopotomoi, were slaughtered, and many Indians still lie nearby in unmarked graves. It is thus fertile ground for the faint battle whoops of fallen warriors and scalped Englishmen, yet no one has heard so much as a whimper from these blood-drenched grounds.

* * * * *

If retribution were the motive, the renowned patriot George Wythe would have cause to return to Richmond in unearthly form to vent his displeasure. For it was at a house on the corner of Fifth and Grace Streets that he was poisoned by a grand nephew seeking his inheritance. Wythe was the brilliant law scholar who numbered among his students, Thomas Jefferson, James Monroe, John Marshall and Henry Clay.

The nephew was foiled in his attempt in that Wythe lingered on, in agonizing pain, for several days before dying. Realizing who had poisoned him, he had time to disinherit his kin, although the man was never convicted of murder. Perhaps Wythe felt this was punishment enough, so there was no need to come back to haunt.

* * * * *

At Tudor Hall in Dinwiddie, outside of Petersburg, Mrs. Thomas Diehl, an octogenarian, tells a colorful story about the ghosts in her home that never were. The house predates the Civil War and its owners fled when some fierce skirmishes were waged in the area. For a time, Tudor Hall served as a hospital for Union soldiers, and according to a legend that has been passed down for generations, some of them still return to march at night across the attic floor.

At least that's what Mrs. Diehl's father used to say, although she admits he was a great tease. One night before she was born, two young women relatives were visiting and spent the night in a room close to the stairway that led to the attic. The stairway is of "perfectly beautiful pine and long and winding."

Mrs. Diehl's father had tantalized them after dinner with the story of the military ghosts, and, coincidentally, that night as they lay in bed they heard a noise that "sounded exactly like a lot of people marching across the attic." They were understandably frightened and called the man of the house who by this time was scared himself.

Together, they finally managed enough courage to investigate. They discovered a saddle that had been placed on the railing above the stairs. It had fallen and the wooden stirrups hit each step on the way down, sounding like marching men across the attic.

Mrs. Diehl says her father was reluctant to talk about the ghosts after that.

* * * * *

Another who has just cause to make an ethereal appearance is Jefferson Davis, President of the Confederate States of America. It was at the White House of the Confederacy, in 1864, that his five-year-old son, Joe, fell from a balcony and was killed. It was a tragedy Davis never fully got over.

There are further reasons for his reappearance. In 1913, his body was exhumed in New Orleans and transported across the South to be reinterred at Hollywood Cemetary. There, the grave of his young son lies at the foot of his own. But apparently Davis found peace at last in Richmond, for all has been quiet through the years both at the White House of the Confederacy and at his burial site in Hollywood Cemetary.

* * * * *

Unquestionably, the most likely spot in all of the city for a haunting, however, is at Jefferson Park Hill, above Marshall and 19th Streets. This is the site of a Chesapeake and Ohio railroad tunnel. It is today filled with sand, its two entrances sealed off and hidden behind a forest of trees and vines.

The tunnel seemed ill-fated from the beginning. As it was being built in the 1870s there was a cave-in and six houses in Jefferson Park collapsed into the pit. But it was a half century later — on October 2, 1925 — that an unforgettable tragedy struck.

It was on this rainy Friday afternoon that a black laborer named Lemy Campbell was working near one entrance to the tunnel. Inside, a large force of men were working on tunnel repairs. Engineer Tom Mason sat inside the cab of a work train locomotive used to switch cars.

Shortly after three p.m., Campbell heard the sound of a brick falling, then another, then another. He looked up and heard a sickening crackling noise along the tunnel roof. As he dashed for safety the roof crashed behind him, mingling the roar of earth, bricks and timber with the anguished screams of trapped men. As the lights in the tunnel flickered and then went out, crew members and laborers alike scrambled for the exits. Some made it out the western entrance, only a few hundred yards away, while others fled toward the eastern entrance, nearly a mile in distance.

In the chaotic blackness, panic ruled. One survivor, quoted at the time in the Richmond *Times Dispatch,* gave a vividly descriptive insight: "Men passed me screaming and fighting. Some of them yelled that they had knives and would cut anybody that got in their way. Others were praying — you never heard such praying...they lost their direction in the darkness...butted their heads into the side walls, fell over the tires and rails and knocked each other down...It was like being in the bottomless pit."

Of the train crew, engineer Mason was trapped in the cab. Fireman B. F. Mosby crawled underneath 10 flat cars and got out of the tunnel only to die that night of burns suffered from the escaping steam of the locomotive. Conductor C. G. McFadden, his arm broken, and brakeman C. S. Kelso, together, made it to safety. Brakeman A. G. Adams, knocked to the ground and stunned by the avalanche of earth, also crawled under the flatcars and made it to daylight. It was hours before an accounting of the laborers could be made. Reports are that two of them were buried alive in the tunnel.

Frantic rescue efforts continued around the clock for nine days, hampered by fresh cave-ins. Finally, on Sunday evening, October 11, shafts sunk by power shovels broke through to the train, torches cut through the steel, and there rescuers found the bolt upright body of the engineer locked in by the brake lever. He had been crushed to death.

Although this happened six decades ago, nagging questions still persist. Are the bodies of the two black laborers still in the tunnel, laying under tons of earth? And were only four people killed in the disaster? Many survivors insisted that several other laborers were taken on just for that day's work. Did they escape, or are they, too, entombed forever?

Such a setting is nearly ideal for the haunting cries of the victims' ghosts. But such cries have never been heard.

THE SKELETON WITH THE TORTOISE SHELL COMB

"...I have been sleeping — and now — now — I am dead."
—The Facts in the Case of M. Valdemar

The first account of the 19th century hauntings of Hawes House in Richmond was published in 1910 by renowned local author Mrs. Edward Terhune, who under the pen name of Marion Harland, wrote the "Lassie" books among others. Subsequently, Margaret DuPont Lee retold the story in her 1930 book, "Virginia Ghosts," and over the years other authors also have referred to this bizarre tale.

Mrs. Terhune, whose maiden name was Mary Virginia Hawes, devoted a chapter of her autobiography, "The Story of My Life," to the intriguing "heroine" who has been called everything from the "Little Gray Lady" to the "Tortoise Shell Ghost." Whatever, it is a richly colorful legend that has not tarnished with time. Here goes.

The Hawes family homestead from the 1840s till 1875 was located at 506 East Leigh Street in Richmond. It was a good sized Colonial brick house, built early in the 19th century, that featured large rooms and long passages. The once extensive and beautiful grounds and gardens, including many large shade trees, slowly gave way to the encroaching demands of a growing city.

Nevertheless, it was on a cold winter night in the late 1840s when the young author-to-be, Virginia Hawes first experienced the ghost that was to make itself well known to the family for nearly 30 years. After entertaining a male guest, Virginia saw him off, locked the front door, stopped by her parents room to say good night, and then, lamp in hand, started across a small passageway that divided the two first floor bedrooms.

The light shone bright in this confined area, and she suddenly gasped as she saw, directly in front of her, what she described as a small woman dressed in gray "glide noiselessly along the wall," and then disappear at the Venetian blinds at the end of the front hall, leading into the reception room beyond. The woman appeared to be small and lithe, with her head bowed in her hands. Peculiarly, she wore a high, carved tortoise shell comb in her hair.

Years later Virginia was to write of the occasion: "I have reviewed the moment and its incident a thousand times to persuade myself that the apparition was an optical illusion or a trick of fancy. The 1,001st attempt results as did the first. I shut my eyes to see — always the one figure, the same motion, the same disappearance. She was dressed in gray; she was small and lithe; her head was bowed upon her hands, and she slipped away, hugging the wall as if in flight, vanishing at the closed door. The door I had heard myself latch itself five minutes ago! It did not open to let her through."

At the time, the sighting terrified Virginia. She immediately went back to her parents' room, entered, and exclaimed, "If there is any such thing as a ghost, I have seen one."

Startled, her father reacted immediately, comforting his daughter. He then walked her to her room and told her to try and sleep. The next morning he called Virginia aside and asked her to keep what she had seen to herself. Odd, Virginia thought.

About a month later she and her father were in the drawing room one evening, talking, when her mother came in excitedly and announced, "I have just seen Virginia's ghost. I saw it in the same place and it went in the same direction. It was all in gray, but something white, like a turban, was wrapped around its head."

Young Virginia could see that the revelation had shocked her father, but he gathered himself and asked them not to speak of the incident again. They abided. But while they remained quiet, the ghost did not. Soonafter, Virginia's younger daughter, Mea, burst into the drawing room at twilight one evening, trembling badly, and proclaimed that "something" had chased her down the stairs. She said whoever or whatever it was — she apparently hadn't seen it — had been in high heel shoes that tapped loudly on the oak stairs as she descended from the upper chamber to the parlor.

Still, Mr. Hawes insisted that no one talk of the occurrences.

Next, Alice Hawes, Virginia's 14-year-old sister, and a cousin visiting the house, encountered the phenomena. Sent to bed at nine o'clock, they instead slipped into the parlor and sat before the fireplace talking for about an hour. When they went back into the hall to go to the bedroom they found it dark. The lamp had burned out.

Brilliant moonlight, however, streamed through the great window on the lower staircase, showering the stairway up to the upper landing. They stared, transfixed, as they saw a "white figure" moving down the steps. At first, they thought it was just one of the boys sneaking down for a glass of water or a snack. The figure appeared to have a trailing nightgown or nightshirt, and it seemed to the girls that there was something white cast over the head.

As the figure moved nearer, the front door suddenly opened and in walked all the boys of the house, back from a nighttime stroll. At the same instant the white thing descending the stairs disappeared before the girls' eyes. Alice said it didn't go backward or forward. It just vanished. Understandably, the girls screamed in unison, arousing everyone in the house.

The next morning, Mr. Hawes called the family together and told them: "It is useless to try to hide from ourselves any longer that there is something wrong with this house. I have known it for a year or more. In fact, we had not lived here three months before I was made aware that some mystery hung about it.

"One windy November night I had gone to bed as usual before your mother. I lay with closed eyes listening to wind and rain when somebody touched my feet." He stressed that it was somebody, not something, before continuing. "Hands were laid lightly upon them; were lifted and laid in the same way on my knees, and so on until they lay more heavily upon my chest and I felt someone was looking in my face. Up to that moment I had not a doubt but that it was your mother arranging the covers to keep out draughts. I opened my eyes to thank her. She was not there! I raised myself on my elbow and looked towards the fireplace. Your mother was deep in her book!

I have never spoken of this even to your mother until this moment. But it has happened to me not 20, but 50 times or more. It is always the same thing. The hands, I have settled in my mind, are those of a small woman, or child. Sometimes the hands rest on my chest a whole minute. Something looks into my face and is gone." Looking at Virginia, Mr. Hawes said: "You can see, my daughter, why I was not incredulous when you brought your ghost upon the scene. I have been on the lookout for further manifestations. By all means do not let the servants hear of this. You girls are old enough to understand that the value of this property would be destroyed were this story to creep abroad. Better burn the house down than attempt to sell it at any time within the next 50 years with a ghost story tagged to it."

Everyone dutifully pledged to remain silent, including, apparently, the ghost, at least for a while. But it resurfaced once more some period later, this time with almost comical overtones. That was when a distant relative, described as a "sanctimonious uncle-in-law" came for a visit. He usually stayed several days at the least; a fact which caused the family some concern because they were expecting other guests and needed the spare bedroom. However, to their surprise, he abruptly announced on the morning after his arrival that he had to leave immediately for Olney.

Later, a relative who lived in Olney was at the Hawes House and asked if the house was haunted. Everyone, as if on cue, acted innocently, and inquired why she would ask such a silly question. "Well," she told them, the uncle "had an awful scare the night he was here. He declared he was standing at the window looking out into the moonlight in the garden when somebody came up behind him and took him by the elbow and turned him clear around! He felt plainly the two hands that grabbed hold of him. He looked under the bed and in the closet. There was nobody in the room but himself, and the door was locked. He said he would not sleep in that room again for one thousand dollars!"

Such is the saga of the "Gray Lady" of Hawes House. Neither Virginia Hawes nor any other member of her family was ever able to determine the identity of the apparition they had seen and felt. Often, such phenomena is closely associated with either the house involved or the family. But no historical tie-in could be found in this case.

A footnote to the story, though, offers some clues. After the death of Mr. Hawes, and the marriage of the sons and daughters, Mrs. Hawes sold the house to St. Paul's Episcopal Church, and it was subsequently converted into an orphanage. During the construction modifications, workmen dug an areaway in front of the premises. Four feet down they unearthed the skeletal remains of a small woman. She lay less than six feet away from the wall of the house and directly under the drawing room window.

And, oh yes, under the woman's skull, workmen found a richly carved tortoise shell comb!

There are some who speculate that the woman was either murdered or at least died under suspicious circumstances. Such a theory is supported by the fact that no sign of a coffin or coffin plate was found. Nor had the woman been buried in a cap or shroud as was common in that day. Also, there were no known interments in that residential district. In fact, the grave had been dug in the front garden so close to the house that it could not be reasonably conceived that the plot was ever part of a family burying ground.

All of this would explain — at least to those who study the common denominators of the supernatural — why the woman continued to haunt Hawes House. She was, in the parlance of ghost followers, in a state of perpetual unrest, either seeking retribution for whatever evil had befallen her, or not gaining that, determined to expose that evil.

Apparently the evacuation of the Hawes family did nothing to deter the woman from continuing to pursue her eerie vigil. For Virginia Hawes later learned from a former neighbor that the manifestations persisted for years afterward at the orphanage. He told her "of a midnight alarm, of screaming children at the occasion of a little gray lady walking between the double row of beds in the dormitory."

THE UNSOLVED RIDDLE OF ROCK CASTLE

"The avenues to death are numerous and strange."
—The Angel of the Odd

Rock Castle, located off Route 600 in Goochland County not far from Tuckahoe Plantation, was named for a high rock bluff overlooking the James River. The first owner of this site of scenic farmlands and woodlands was Charles Fleming of St. Peter's Parish, New Kent County. On July 12, 1718, he received a Royal Grant for 1,430 acres. Historians are not exactly sure when the small, five-bay, story-and-a-half house was built, but they speculate, with reasonable confidence, that it was between 1718 and 1732. Col. William Byrd II of Westover Plantation in Charles City County mentions Rock Castle in his book "Progress to the Mines," indicating that it was completed prior to 1732.

In one manner of speaking the house — which is now known as the Queen Anne Cottage — was "lost" for a period of years. The Flemings continued to own and live at Rock Castle until it was sold out of the family in 1798. It passed through several hands before being sold, along with 576 acres, to John Rutherfoord for the princely sum of $6,631. Rutherfoord, incidentally, served as Governor of Virginia for exactly one year — from March 31, 1841 to March 31, 1842.

It was his only son and heir, John Coles Rutherfoord, who "hid" the original structure by building an Italianate front on it, having been impressed with Italian villas he had seen during a grand tour of Europe following his graduation from college. He also supervised the laying out of the famous garden on the grounds.

Ownership of Rock Castle changed hands many more times until it was purchased in 1935 by James Osborne, author of "The Greatest Norman Conquest." It was he and his wife who "rediscovered" the original building when they planned to put up a Norman Manor house on the property. As carpenters started dismantling the Italianate style villa, they "found" the old Queen Anne Cottage. This was carefully taken apart and re-erected facing the garden.

That the old house survived at all is close to a miracle, and presents some interesting historical vignettes. In 1781, for example, Lt. Col. Banastre Tarteton stopped at the site on his return from the unsuccessful attempt to capture Thomas Jefferson and the Virginia legislators at Charlottesville. His men set fire to the house, but servants extinguished it with little damage resulting. Then, in 1865, a marauding company of Union cavalry under General Philip Sheridan forced their way into Rock Castle and "destroyed everything they could not carry away." Thus it is somewhat remarkable that this quaint house, with its hand-carved staircase, panelled wainscoating, and beautiful mantels remains intact today.

It also has persevered through a number of hauntings and strange occurrences, which allude to, but do not explain, some dark tragedies of bygone days. These are of more modern vintage. In the late 1930s Mr. and Mrs. Philip Mason Cabell owned Rock Castle and reported hearing frequent footsteps in the house.

Sometime during this era a psychic came to hold a seance. As several guests held hands while sitting around a card table, the table allegedly "jumped high in the air." Next, a code alphabet was established. One rap for "A," two for "B," etc. Sometime after midnight, a word, or rather a name was spelled out — "Pierson" — but no one recognized it. The next day Mrs. Calvert Osborne (her husband's parents were the

Cabells) asked her neighbor, James Rutherfoord of Ben Lomond, if he had ever heard of anyone named Pierson. He told her a man by that name had once owned Rock Castle, but had been killed in a car accident one night while driving to Ben Lomond. That had been, Rutherfoord thought, about 1922. Curiously, Mrs. Osborne's husband, too, was killed when his car smashed into a tree on the old River Road.

* * * * *

Not far from Rock Castle, on the north side of the River Road in Goochland County about two and a half miles west of Manakin, is Joe Brooke Plantation. The history of this land dates to 1703, when a Royal Patent covering 2,700 acres was issued to John Woodson. His son later sold 1,750 acres to Thomas Randolph, builder of Tuckahoe, and subsequently the property exchanged hands many times over the next 150 years.

No one knows how old the Joe Brooke house is, although it is believed it was built by a Randolph, possibly William, sometime prior to his death in 1745. This is speculated because in the late 1930s, while repairs were being made to the roof of the large brick house, a contractor saw a brick on the roof side of the west chimney near the roofline which had a workman's initials scratched on it and the date 1761.

There also is a ghost at Joe Brooke house who may date to that era, because tales are told of the sighting of a "figure of a man in knee breeches" who walks about the house on moonlit nights. Who is he and why does he haunt? The answer may lie in a ghastly discovery made by workmen some years ago. While doing repair work on the central chimney, they were digging under the floor. There, they discovered the skeleton of a man. No hair was found on the skull, indicating the body had been there a long, long time.

THE
GHOST BRIGADE
OF CENTRE HILL

"...A great hero, in the heat of combat, not perceiving that he had been fairly killed, continued to fight valiently, dead as he was."
—How to Write a Blackwood Article

Although encroached upon by the entrapments of the modern world, Centre Hill stands today, as it has for well over a century and a half, as the dominating architectural showpiece of Petersburg. It vividly recalls the antebellum splendor and prosperity of the old city. One early visitor to the mansion described it as a "superb" building offering a "grand and imposing view," and the wife of John Tyler, 10th President of the United States, said "the place is on a large and in some respects a really grand scale."

The grounds themselves are historic, for before the house was built, they served as a muster ground for the militia. It was, in fact, from this site that the famous company of Petersburg volunteers departed to distinguish themselves in battle in the War of 1812, and thus earn for Petersburg the title, "The Cockade City of the Union."

Perhaps this requires a little explanation, which is provided by Dr. James Bailey, city historian. "This is in reference to the fact that in the War of 1812, the volunteers marched to Ohio and fought with great valor at Fort Meigs," Dr. Bailey says. "During this period they wore cockades in their hats, which actually were black leather rosettes. In giving recognition to their heroism, President James Madison made the comment that Petersburg was the "Cockade of the Union," meaning the ornament of the Union as typified by the men who wore the rosettes in their hat. The city is still known by that soubriquet, and is duly proud of it.

Centre Hill was built in 1823 for Robert Bolling, great grandson of the emigrant Robert Bolling, founder of a well-known Virginia family. Situated in a beautifully planted and enclosed park of over eight acres, it was constructed in "generous proportions" of oversize brick in Flemish bond, and is architecturally referred to as a "transitional Greek Revival style house."

Magnificent wolfhounds of Carrara marble guard the entrance to the columned portico, and the interior is adorned with hand-carved woodwork and lavish cornices. Remnants of a tunnel connecting the house with the Appomattox River can still be seen from the lower level of the house. It was built for the convenience of guests, mostly James River plantation owners who arrived there by barge. A mineral spring on the grounds supplied water for the city before the establishment of the municipal waterworks in 1856.

Like other mansions of its size and prominence, Centre Hill has played host to its share of dignitaries over the years, including Abraham Lincoln. After the Confederate evacuation of the city, which ended the ten-months siege of Petersburg, the house became the headquarters of Major General G. L. Hartsuff, district commander for the Union. Lincoln met with him here on April 7, 1865. When the subject of rent was discussed, Lincoln said "our batteries have made rent enough here already."

President William Howard Taft visited Centre Hill on May 19, 1909, upon the occasion of the unveiling of a monument. The house went through a number of owners before Edgar S. Bowling presented it to the U.S. Government in 1937 for the purpose of transforming it into a museum. This was delayed by the advent of World War II, when Centre Hill was used as headquarters for the Petersburg chapter of the American Red Cross.

It was officially opened as a Civil War era museum in 1950, and included exhibits and displays depicting the decisive and dramatic events in the history of Petersburg — Civil War portraits, uniforms, swords, pistols, shells, projectiles, rare maps, and the Confederate flag which flew above Hustings Courthouse until the day of the surrender. Centre Hill later was turned over to the City of Petersburg and today is a major tourist attraction.

With such an illustrious history it is not surprising that the mansion is associated with some colorful ghostly legends. "Oh, yes, there are some interesting stories," says Dr. Bailey. One of the most common concerned "a beautifully dressed lady" who frequently sat at the second story window over the front door. She was seen by many passersby, but no one ever knew who she was. This occurred in the latter years of the 19th century. Once, during this time, a child living in the house told his mother of a "pretty lady" who had visited him during the night, sat on the side of his bed, held his hand, and talked to him. He indicated that he could see right through her, meaning she gave a transparent appearance. The description he gave perfectly matched that of the woman others had seen in the window.

Mrs. Campbell Pryor, a direct descendent of the builder of Centre Hill lived in the house in the 1880s and 1890s, and told of the spectral playing of a little melodeon that stood in a corner of the library. "Many, many times," she said, "familiar airs have been heard played by invisible hands, as no mortal was in the room."

Her husband also experienced the strange phenomena. He once tried to use as a bed chamber a small room on the first floor near an office, but apparently the ghost, or whatever it was, felt this room belonged to it. Everytime Mr. Campbell retired and the lights were turned out, "invisible hands jerked the coverings off the bed and threw them onto the middle of the floor!"

But the oddest manifestation of all was the return of the troop of soldiers, presumably Civil War veterans, who for a number of years in succession tramped through the house precisely at 7:30 p.m. each January 24th. So regular was their procession, that the house owners at the time invited friends and neighbors in to witness the eerie spectacle.

This was best expressed by Margaret DuPont Lee in her 1930 book, "Virginia Ghosts." "On that day of the year," Mrs. DuPont wrote, "the clock pointing to the half hour, the door leading into the office was heard to open. Then a noise such as of a regiment of soldiers marching! The clank as of sabres suggested the occupation of those tramping along the passage; up the stair and into a room over the office. After about twenty minutes the sound was again heard descending the steps, crossing the hall, then finally the slamming of a door and all was quiet."

THE CATASTROPHE AT THE CAPITOL

"The very air from the South seemed to be redolent with death."
—*The Sphinx*

They are heard only late at night, the sounds. Some say they are but the normal creaks, groans and wind whistles of an old building. But there are others, including members of the security force, who swear there are voices; soft muted voices sobbing and moaning in the darkened stillness of the State Capitol Building.

Certainly, if the sounds are voices there is good reason for their anguished cries.

Thomas Jefferson conceived the plan for the Capitol, patterning it after the Maison Carrée, a Roman temple built in Nimes, France, in the first century after Christ. It was the first public building in the New World constructed in the Classical Revival style of architecture, and is the second oldest working Capitol in the United States. It has been in continuous use since October 1788.

According to the official Capitol brochure, the structure drew high praise from its earliest days. "Even in its present unfinished state," wrote a visitor in 1796, "the building is, beyond comparison, the finest, the most noble, and the greatest in all America." The brochure calls it, "a magnificent monument to Virginia's past." Here, in the grand rotunda, is the state's most treasured work of art, a life-sized statue of George Washington carved in Carrara marble by the brilliant French artist Jean Antoine Houdon in 1788. There also are

busts of the seven other Virginia-born U.S. Presidents as well as a bronze statue of Robert E. Lee by Rudolph Evans.

Ironically, although the building served as the Capitol of the Confederacy from 1861 to 1865, it escaped damage during the Civil War, only to suffer a tragedy of enormous proportions five years later. The date was April 27, 1870. It was Richmond's second major catastrophe in less than 60 years, the other being the ruinous theatre fire of 1811.

The circumstances leading up to it were these: Although military rule had ended, there was still confusion and turmoil in the governing of the city and state. The general assembly authorized the governor to appoint a new city council, which he did. The council elected Henry Ellyson, publisher of the Richmond *Dispatch*, as the new mayor.

However, George Chahoon, who had been serving as mayor, refused to relinquish his office. This led to what has been described as "a chaotic state of affairs," as the two rival forces struggled to gain control. The dispute got nasty and eventually wound up in the Virginia Supreme Court of Appeals, which convened to hear the case on April 27, 1870.

Everybody who was anybody in the city, jammed into the

Capitol that day to hear the proceedings in what was to be a landmark decision. Hundreds of participants and spectators shoehorned into the courtroom, on an upper floor, and overflowed the gallery.

Minutes before the court convened there was a "loud cracking noise and then pandemonium. The gallery floor collapsed under the weight of the overflow crowd, and bricks, iron bars, plaster, planks, furniture and a mass of people fell onto the courtroom floor below. Under the impact of this tremendous amount of debris and humanity, the floor buckled and gave way, careening to the ground floor some 40 feet below.

Scores of people were crushed to death immediately, while others suffocated under the huge cloud of dust from tons of plaster that made it all but impossible to see anything. Many were buried alive under the rubble. The pain and suffering were incalculable, and there were screams, cries and moans everywhere. The lucky ones ran, walked or crawled outside and fell, gasping, to the lawn.

The fire alarm was sounded and firemen, police and other rescuers arrived, but it took hours to disentangle the bodies. Survivors were carried out to the lawn covered with blood and lime dust to the point of being unrecognizable. One eye witness said they looked more like "bloody ghosts" than human beings. Rescuers commandeered passing carriages, hacks and other vehicles to convey the injured to hospitals. Every doctor and nurse in Richmond was summoned, and when word of the disaster spread, wives, relatives and friends rushed to the Capitol, adding to the anguish and chaos. Some did not learn of their loved ones fate for a considerable period of time.

Grown men cried openly at the ghastly scene and one witness was moved to write, "I can't dwell upon these awful scenes, they were so heartrending, so appalling that they unman me when I recall them."

In all, 62 men lost their lives — just 10 less than the number killed in the 1811 fire. More than 250 were injured, some dreadfully, their bodies mangled and their bones crushed. The victims included many prominent citizens, among them

Patrick Henry's grandson and several well-known lawyers. Fortunately, the House of Delegates was not in session, otherwise the list would have been even more lengthy.

A curious twist of fate spared the members of the Supreme Court of Appeals. The proceedings were delayed for 15 minutes as the judges conferred over some changes in their written opinion of the case. They were just starting into the court room from an adjoining conference room when the gallery floor gave way, and they stood on the very brink of the "awful abysm."

Once again, Richmond was plunged into municipal mourning, just five years after the city had been sacked and burned. Business houses closed and crepe was displayed widely. Resolutions were introduced in the Senate calling for the demolition of the Capitol, and the erection of a new one, but it finally was decided to strengthen and rebuild the existing building.

Ellyson eventually was declared the rightful mayor, and Chahoon later was sent to prison on forgery charges. He was pardoned by the governor on the condition that he leave the state. In time, the Capitol was rebuilt and the business of running the Commonwealth went on.

But although more than a century has passed, and the tragedy is but a black-bordered footnote in history, some say the eerie cry of mournful voices, muted under tons of debris, can still be heard in the hallowed corridors of the Capitol.

THE UNHAPPY BRIDE OF TUCKAHOE

"Today I wear these chains and am here! Tomorrow I shall be fetterless — but where?"

—*The Imp of the Perverse*

"Considered by architectural historians to be the finest existing early 18th century plantation in America, Tuckahoe stands today in its virtually undisturbed setting on a bluff overlooking the James River valley." Those words are the lead-in to a brochure on this truly splendid mansion located about 15 miles west of Richmond off River Road in Goochland County.

For countless generations writers have outdone themselves heaping superlatives on the house and grounds. Said one: "Not only is the house priceless because of its completeness, but it contains some of the most important architectural ideas of the early Georgian Period." Another wrote: "Despite the spread of Richmond's suburbs it retains a marvellous sense of remoteness. A long, straight drive leads through woods for nearly a mile before breaking into a clearing in which the house stands neatly on axis, surrounded by spreading lawns and noble trees."

One author described the entrance into Tuckahoe in these elegant terms: "The oldest of these trees in their lusty age extend arms farther afield than in their youth, their naked

Ghost Walk at Tuckahoe.

trunks standing stiff and upright, so like the pipes of some cathedral organ that one would not start at the sound of deep, reverential tones coming along the lane. It is most impressive.

"Down the lofty nave of this forest cathedral gleams, at the end, under the open sky, the old, white gateway which bars the lane from the lawn. And straight ahead in the distance, upon a little rise of ground, the old house stands like some fading seventeenth-century picture shut away in its immediate world. Approaching it through the old gateway, one will never forget the picture, especially if the season be spring. Hoary-headed elm trees and clouds of golden daffodils literally surround it. Goldfinches and mocking-birds twitter a welcome, and, girdling all, the James River in the distance. The daffodils bend and sway, seeming to beckon one nearer, and the hospitable face of the old house wears the same warm welcome it wore in colonial days."

The name Tuckahoe, according to one 17th century historian, comes from the Indian word "Tockawaugh," which was an edible root found in the area. It was "of the greatness and taste of a potatoe, which passeth a fiery purgation before they may eate it being poison while it is raw."

The oldest portion of the house, the north wing, says a Virginia Historic Landmarks Commission report, was built by Thomas Randolph, perhaps as early as 1712. This means it predates such other famous James River plantation homes as Westover, Carter's Grove and Shirley. Thomas was the son of William Randolph of Turkey Island (1651-1711), who had emigrated to Virginia about 1673. One account states he had accumulated, "by headright, purchase, grants, legacies and other means," vast tracts of land by 1705, including 10,000 acres in Henrico County.

He set each of his seven sons up with their own estate: William at Chatsworth; Isham at Dungeness; Richard at Curles; Sir John at Tazewell Hall; Henry at Longfield; Edward at Bremo; and Thomas, the second eldest, at Tuckahoe.

The mansion, built in part of colonial brick and in part of wood, is of unusual design. There are two major wings, each 25 feet deep and 40 feet long, connected by a hall 24 feet wide and 40 feet long. Arched doorways open at either end into the wings — giving the house the shape of the letter H. It is thus in effect two houses in one, connected by the great hall. It is believed to have been modeled after the Virginia Capitol building in Williamsburg, which was erected on such an H-plan in 1699.

While the exterior of Tuckahoe may not be as imposing as some of its sister plantation homes — one writer said, "it boasts no pretension to grandeur" — the interior is indeed magnificent. It has superb paneled walls, and the stairways are outstanding examples of the early Georgian period. The balusters are elaborately turned and spiraled. The north stairway has a principal newel post in the form of a Corinthian colonette carved with vines and flowers and square fluted intermediate posts. The notably fine brackets, which are almost identical with those at Carter's Grove near Williamsburg, are scrolled and carved with acanthus and five-petaled blossoms. The first floor plan is repeated on the second, where there were originally four large bedrooms and two halls. The mantels throughout the house date from the early 19th century, but the marble fireplace facing with flat lintel and keystone in the east bedroom of the north wing is original. All over the house the woodwork is elaborate and beautiful. The north end paneled rooms show especially refined cornices.

Probably unique in American architecture are the rare outbuildings along "plantation street." They include a kitchen, slaves' quarters, a smokehouse, storage structures, and a small, one-room, one-story school house.

One 18th century guest of Tuckahoe, Baron von Closen, wrote in 1782: ". . . After a delicious supper, served with all possible elegance, we were led by the son of the house to our

apartments, which were worthy of a Prince's Palace; every piece of furniture was exquisitely beautiful, of mahogany or rosewood, with very beautiful mirrors. I absolute had to force myself to sleep in a damask bed; the general's apartment was all done in velvet and gold, and his bed was decorated like a Feast-Day!''

As impressive as the physical features and furnishings of the house were, Tuckahoe was equally renowned for the hospitality its owners lavished on guests. Said the Marquis de Chastellux, who visited there in the 1780s: "The Virginians have the reputation, and with reason, of living nobly in their houses, and of being hospitable; they give strangers not only a willing, but a liberal, reception." And Thomas Anbury penned, in his "Travels Through the Interior Parts of North America" in 1789: "I spent a few days at Colonel Randolph's at Tuckahoe, at whose house the usual hospitality of the country prevailed."

Thomas Randolph died, in 1729, willing Tuckahoe to his only son, William, who was a burgess for Goochland. He died in 1745, leaving a large estate. He bequeathed 1,200 pounds in sterling — a fortune in those days — to each of his two daughters, and requested that Peter Jefferson come to Tuckahoe as an overseer and guardian, and hired a tutor to teach his young son, Thomas Mann Randolph. Jefferson did, bringing with him his young son, Thomas, who spent seven of his first nine years at the plantation going to classes with the Randolph children in the tiny school house on the grounds.

Tuckahoe remained in the possession of the Randolph family until 1830, when it was sold and subsequently passed through a succession of owners. The current "squires" of the land are the A. B. Thompsons.

As with many of the great plantation homes in Virginia, especially along the James, and including Brandon, Berkeley, Carter's Grove, Westover and Shirley — Tuckahoe has its share of ghostly legends, some of which have been experienced by highly credible witnesses and fairly well documented. Others are more sketchy.

There is, for example, the story of the itinerant peddler. In days gone by these horse and wagon forerunners to the modern traveling salesmen used to ply their trades to the great outlying plantations, selling everything from primitive cosmetics and miracle healing substances to trimmings and dress goods. Allegedly a lace peddler arrived at Tuckahoe one day to vend his wares, but instead got into a fierce altercation with a member of the household and was murdered. He is said to reappear at times, seeking retribution, in the southeast çhamber of the house.

There also is "a little gray lady" at the site. Such ladies seem to be fairly common in old Virginia circles. There is a rather well known one at Sherwood Forest in Charles City County, home of President John Tyler. A Tyler descendent believes the specters of gray ladies, or rather ladies in gray, stem from the fact that most servants in the great houses along the James wore gray uniforms.

Anyway, in a book titled "Historical Gardens of Virginia," published in 1923, there is reference to a "dainty little Gray Lady (incidentally all of spectral gray ladies appear to be small for some reason) who, when the midnight hour has come, steps gently out from a cupboard in the lovely old 'Burnt Room' to mingle with the mortals for awhile." A second published reference to this particular phenomena relates to Mrs. Richard S. Allen, whose husband, Joseph, bought Tuckahoe in 1850. She and a friend reportedly were standing in the dining room one day when "both of them saw distinctly the figure of a small woman in gray enter through the hall door and pass out the little entry door leading to the outer kitchen."

Mrs. Allen may have been mediumistic, because other strange things happened to her during her tenure at Tuckahoe. A Richmond *Times-Dispatch* article written more than 50 years ago recalled the time Mrs. Allen was sitting in the upstairs hall unpacking a box. The only other person around was a maid who was washing windows. Mrs. Allen heard someone call her name, "Jennie." She looked up, saw no one and continued her work. Then the call was repeated "in loud and anxious tones." The mystery voice fairly bellowed, "Jennie! Jennie!" This aroused her to her feet, and she hurried into the room where the maid was to see if something was wrong, knowing that only that would cause the maid to call her by her first name. But she found the servant quietly washing a window. Just then a loud crash startled them both. They raced back into the room where Mrs. Allen had been and found that a large portion of the ceiling had fallen and completely demolished the very chair upon which she had been sitting!

There is one other episode involving the Allens which is worthy of retelling. One evening family members and some guests were amusing themselves with a Planchette. This was a 19th century predecessor to the Ouija board. It is a small board supported on casters at two points and a vertical pencil at a third, and believed to produce automatic writing when lightly touched by the finger.

Anyway, someone asked "who is your master," and the pencil spelled out "the devil." Then the question was posed, is Tuckahoe haunted? The answer was not only emphatic, but descriptive: "Yes, the red room upstairs, and it has an odd panel in the wall." This triggered a dash up the stairs to this room where indeed an odd panel was discovered that had not been previously noticed.

Then it was remembered that years earlier a traveling man who had spent a night in that room said he had been awakened in the middle of the night by a rocking chair rocking violently back and forth. He got up, lit a lamp and saw the chair rocking, but there was no one in it. No window was open, so no draft could have set the chair in motion. He went back to sleep only to be reawakened by the same manifestation. This was enough for him. He hastily dressed, packed and vacated the house, telling a perplexed servant along the way out that nothing on earth would induce him to stay in that room again.

There is an earlier tale, too, about a dream of a "fragile wraith" which led to "one of Tuckahoe's most loved chatelaines" being brought to preside in the house. It was the dream of Thomas Mann Randolph III, great-grandson of the builder of the house. After the death of his first wife, he envisioned one evening that a young lady opened a closet door in his bedroom and brought him a glass of water. The next day he spoke of the apparition and said the face was so clear that if he ever saw it again he would instantly recognize it. Accordingly, years later he did meet the woman of his dreams in Patterson, New Jersey, proposed to her, married her, and brought her back to the mansion!

Since moving into Tuckahoe a few years ago, Tad and Sue Thompson, a young modern couple with three small children, have either heard of, or personally experienced a few strange things at the house. "I guess the most distinct one," says Sue, "was one time in the middle of the night I woke up and heard the vague hum of voices downstairs, and a tinkling sound, like glasses or a chandelier. As I became fully awake, it sounded more like a party was going on, a really happy one. I roused Tad and said 'do you hear that,' and he said he did. It definitely sounded like a party, but it was muted. It was like it was far off somewhere. Tad went down to look but he didn't find anything. I'm not a great believer in this sort of thing, but it was very real that night. We heard something!

"There have been a couple of other things," Sue Thompson continues. "Once I saw someone or something in white at the little school house building. The door was open and I thought it was Tad. But it wasn't, and I never knew who it was. Other times I feel like I hear a baby crying in another part of the house, when I know all my children are accounted for."

Sue also tells of a time in April 1982 when an English woman friend of hers was visiting the plantation. "She went to the laundry room while I was in the kitchen, and she came back a few minutes later and appeared a littled startled. She asked me if I had been in the laundry room, but I told her I hadn't. She just stared at me. Then she told me she had seen something in there."

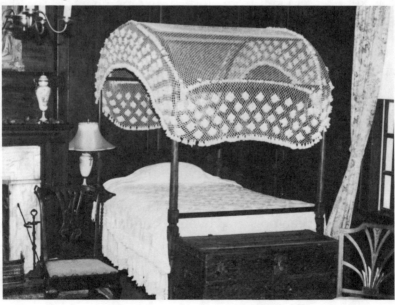

On another occasion some friends were leaving Tuckahoe early one morning when they stopped to check a tire on the car. As they did, they happened to look toward the house. "They said they saw a figure in white near the garden toward the tool shed," Sue explains. "They said it was sort of hovering above the garden."

And one day Tad was showing a reporter about the house. They had just left one upstairs bedroom and crossed over to the Red Room when they heard a crash in the first room. It sounded like something had slid across a table and fallen to the floor, but when they went back in to look nothing was amiss. Yet the sound of the crash could be clearly heard on the reporter's tape recorder when they played it back.

Sue has a possible theory. "My feeling is that if there is an unhappy ghost at Tuckahoe, it might be Judith Randolph. She's buried here. She had a tragic life." The story behind this, as chronicled in "Mistress Nancy," and other books on Tuckahoe and the Randolph family, is that Judith was married to Richard Randolph many generations ago. There was an alleged scandal. Judith's younger sister, Nancy, was said to have had an affair with Richard and became pregnant. This was kept secret even from close family members. When the child arrived, delivered at another plantation by servants, it was either born dead or was killed, and the whole affair was hushed up. Nevertheless, ugly rumors circulated, so to clear up the matter, Richard, who was accused of snuffing out the baby's life, stood trial for murder. He was acquitted, as was Nancy, by a brilliant defense devised by none other than Patrick Henry.

Judith Randolph, however, later had a son who was born deaf. Deeply religious, she believed that in keeping quiet about what actually had transpired, the Lord was using this deafness to punish her, and she lived for years with guilt. Richard later died unexpectedly, and some have offered that he may have been poisoned by Judith. All of this leads Sue to wonder that if one of the ghosts of Tuckahoe is a sad one, could it be the return of Judith who grew up there so many years ago?

But by far the best known of all spirits at Tuckahoe is the

"distressed bride with flowing hair" who, dressed in wedding veil and satin gown, wrings her hands as she "rushes along the Ghost Walk." This walk is a charming vista down a turfed alley lined with old fashioned or suffruticosa box, named in behalf of this spectral presence seen by many for more than 200 years. The legend is that she is running away from a husband she was forced to marry who was three times her age.

One account, in a faded newspaper clip published decades ago, tells of "a sad little ghost, whose tragedy is a matter of family record." She had been married when very young, and much against her own wishes, to a bridgegroom many years her senior. "Shortly after her marriage, she died, presumably of that ailment dear in the memories of our ancestors — a broken heart — and lies in the family burial ground on the estate. We can let our fancy weave a very pretty story of an attractive if impecunious lover, whom her family would not permit her to marry rather than sacrificing her youth and beauty to age and wealth, an old familiar story."

Actually, we can do more than fancy that, because the facts in this case were set down in an absorbing monograph on Tuckahoe Plantation by Jessie Ball Thompson Krusen in 1975. From this we learn that sometime in the early 1730s one of the Randolph daughters named Mary, breaking with her family's wishes, married her uncle's overseer. His name was Isham and he apparently was not well liked by the landed gentry of the day.

Mary was, in fact, sternly censured by none less than Colonel William Byrd II, master of Westover and a longtime close family friend of the Randolphs. Byrd commented on what he viewed as an ill-advised union in this manner, as quoted by Ms. Krusen: "Besides the meanness of this mortal's (the overseer's) aspect, the man has not one visible qualification, except imprudence, to recommend him to a female's inclinations. But there is sometimes such a charm in that Hibernian endowment, that frail women can't withstand it, though it stand alone without any other recommendation. Had she run away with a gentleman or a pretty fellow, there might have been some excuse for her, though he were of inferior fortune: but to stoop to a dirty plebeian without any kind of merit is the lowest prostitution. I found the family justly enraged at it and though I had more good nature than to join in her condemnation, yet I could devise no excuse for so senseless a prank as this young gentlewoman had played."

Ms. Krusen adds that the "unfortunate Mary" was later brought home and forced to marry the much older Mr. James Keith, thus she speculates that it is Mary's pitiable figure that is seen wringing her hands as she flees her elderly husband along Ghost Walk.

THE RAVEN'S LAST READING

"Quoth the Raven, 'Nevermore' "

—The Raven

No book on the ghosts of Richmond would be complete without at least a mention of that master of mystery and the macabre who spent so much of his life in the city, and wrote with such eloquence of tombs and hauntings and mad dreams — Edgar Allan Poe. And surely there is just cause for his spectral return, for his personal life was filled with torment and tragedy.

There was the death of his actress mother, Elizabeth, when he was but three years old. There was his ill-fated love affair with Elmira Shelton, who many speculate may have been the Lenore of his famous poem. During his lifetime he visited some of the haunted houses described in this volume, and he is said to have worshipped at Monumental Church, site of one of Richmond's worst disasters — the horrible theatre fire of 1811. Then there were his battles with drugs and alcohol, which produced nightmarish states of untold horror in his mind.

One would logically assume that Poe's ghost might surface in the vicinity of St. John's Church. It is here that his mother was buried. And across and down the street is the house in which Elmira Shelton lived. But that is not the case. Nor are there any ethereal legends associated with the old Allan home that once stood at 14th and Tobacco Alley, or at the site of the Exchange Hotel, where he gave his last public reading.

The same is true at the Poe Museum on East Main Street, unless one takes literally the words of Emmie Ferguson Farrar, author of "Old Virginia Houses Along the James." She wrote of the museum: "About these (Poe's) objects so lovingly collected, seems to hover the spirit of the great poet; one feels his presence in them...they evoke memories of his passionate, tragic life and the strange dreams and visions he transmuted into unearthly beauty of words and rhythm."

Rather, it is at Talavera, 2315 West Grace Street, that the "presence" of the brilliant and troubled poet and author may have been felt. The hedge word "may" is used here advisedly, because while there have been a number of credible witnesses to the infrequent appearance of a male ghost at this house, no one can say for sure whether or not it is Poe's spirit that is occasionally glimpsed, heard and felt. Still, there is reason enough for Poe to effect his return here.

Talavera was built in 1838 by Thomas Talley and was originally a farm of 25 acres. Richmond historian Mary Winfield Scott once said, "Talavera stands as a vestigial link to the rural farm setting that was once the near West End of Richmond." During the Civil War, the house was surrounded by

fortifications and all of the outbuildings were destroyed. It became, in the words of one pre-war resident, a "desolate abode... In place of the pleasant, smiling home, there stood a bare and lonely house in the midst of encircling fortifications, still bristling with dismantled gun carriages... All the beautiful trees which had made it so attractive — even the young cedar of Lebanon, which had been our pride — were gone; greenhouses, orchard, vineyard, everything, had been swept away, leaving only a dead level, overgrown with broom-straw, amidst which were scattered rusty bayonets..."

That resident was Susan Archer Talley, the daughter of Thomas Talley. She was a writer, poetess and friend of Poe. Not only that, but Poe's sister, Rosalie, lived on an adjoining farm owned by the MacKenzies. Their house was known as Duncan Lodge and was located at a site on Broad and Allan Streets where an old Sears store once stood.

Poe frequently visited Susan Talley at Talavera, and reputedly gave his last known private reading of "The Raven" there on September 25th, 1849. Miss Talley said "his impressive delivery held the company spellbound," and apparently frightened a number of the family servants. When Poe extended his arm during the reading and "cried with awful vehemence" as he quoted the line, 'Get thee back into the tempest and the Night's Plutonian shore!' the servants scampered out of the parlor and retreated to the back of the house. Poe left town the next day for Baltimore and died in that city on October 7, less than two weeks later.

In 1975, a local group called the Young Preservationists bought the house and began plans to renovate it. Several residents there have, over the years, experienced a number of psychic manifestations, leading to the speculative theory that it might be Poe who returns. Talavera is said to be the last standing house in Richmond which he visited.

"A lot of people who have lived here believe the house to be haunted," says Sergei Troubetzkoy, who resides in the spacious downstairs apartment. "Most of them were not aware of anything out of the ordinary when they moved in. In fact, I made it a point of not telling them about the ghost so as not to influence them in any way," he says. Troubetzkoy, it might be added, is a fervent admirer of Poe.

He recalls that shortly after moving into Talavera, he was painting his apartment one day when he distinctly heard footsteps in the entrance foyer. "I felt someone there," he says, but there was no one in evidence. Two friends appeared at his door a short time later and one remarked, "There's a ghost behind you." He said it was a male ghost.

A man in an upstairs apartment once felt something strange for several nights in succession. He claimed that each time he went to bed, something climbed in bed alongside him, and the pillow depressed beneath the head of whatever it was. Other tenants have felt icy cold chills at odd times, even in the heat of summer, and pet owners have said their dogs have gone crazy in the house on occasion. A reporter for Richmond Magazine came out to investigate, only to find her tape recorder "died" while she was in the house, never to work again.

Troubetzkoy says everyone agrees that the ghost is that of a man, and that he is friendly. "Of course," he adds, "we'd like to think he's the ghost of Poe."

CHAPTER 30

THE PSYCHIC WONDERS OF HAW BRANCH

". . .a female voice from its recesses broke suddenly upon the night, in one wild, hysterical, and long-continued shriek."
—The Assignation

"A portrait taken after death."
—Tamerlane

The spirits seem to have settled down at last at Haw Branch Plantation, 35 miles southwest of Richmond. And that is something, because this historic home in Amelia County, Virginia, has probably had more manifestations of psychic phenomena than any other house in the greater Richmond area, if not the entire state.

These have included such familiar forms as: footsteps in the night; the sounds of heavy falling objects; the spectral form of a woman at night; and the recurrent fragrance of attar of roses in an upstairs bedroom. But at Haw Branch, there also have been some rarer occurrences, too. There is, for example, the blood curdling scream of a woman, which happens only on specific dates, at six month intervals. There is the eerie swooping of a giant sized bird with at least a six foot wing span. And most strange of all are the stories behind the portraits. There are two. One, inexplicably, turned from charcoal black and white to full color. The other is a painting